ICONS OF MERCY

Letters from
a Hermitage to Priests
(And to the World)

by
Father George W. Kosicki, C.S.B.

Faith

Published by
FAITH PUBLISHING COMPANY
P.O. Box 237
Milford, Ohio 45150

Published by Faith Publishing Company

For additional copies write:

Faith Publishing Company
P.O. Box 237
Milford, Ohio 45150

Copyright 1990 Faith Publishing Company

Library of Congress Catalog Card No.: 90-080303

ISBN: Applied for.

All rights reserved. No part of this book may be reproduced or transmitted in any form without the written permission of the publisher. For information, address Faith Publishing Company, P.O. Box 237, Milford, Ohio 45150

TABLE OF CONTENTS

	Page
Dedication	v
Acknowledgments	vii
Foreword	ix

Letter:
1. Something More Is Needed! 1
2. The Grace of Solitude 4
3. Now is the Time for Mercy 7
4. The Father of Mercies 11
5. Trust in the Lord 14
6. More Trust 17
7. A New Love for Priests 21
8. Unity of Bishop and Priests 23
9. The Grace of Sonship 27
10. Apostles of Mercy 33
11. Martyrdon 36
12. Mary, Mother of God and my Mother 38
13. Total Baptism in Christ Jesus 45
14. The Priority of Presence to the Father 49
15. The Priest as Icon of Jesus 52
16. The Priest as Intercessor 56
17. The Mystery of Mercy 59
18. The Priest as Victim with Christ for Others 64
19. The Identity of the Priest 77
20. Lamentation 83
21. A Mysterious, Heavenly Priesthood 89

22. Moving On! 93
23. The Priest as a Man of Thanksgiving 97
24. Sin is the Issue 99
25. The Presence of the Priest as Eucharist 102
26. Hastening the Day of the Lord 107
27. Division of East and West 111
28. The Marian Movement of Priests 116
29. We Need a Married Priesthood
    [i.e., Married to the Lord!] 125
30. Need of Knowing Jesus Christ
    and Baptism in the Holy Spirit 129
31. Of Solitude, Teams, and Fraternity 135
32. The Heart of the Priest 141
33. Devotion to the Divine Mercy 150
34. The Priest as Mystery of Mercy and Mary 158
35. An Epilogue: God's Fascinating Ways 162

DEDICATION

To Father Edward L. Scheuerman, brother priest, friend, and a Barnabas (*Acts* 4:2); And to my brother priests.

May these letters on the mystery of mercy and Mary enrich your lives.

George W. Kosicki, C.S.B.

ACKNOWLEDGMENTS

I want to express my deepest thanks and appreciation to the community of hermits at Holy Family Hermitage, Father Charles, Brother Basil and Brother Paul and for Father Michael, Major of the Camaldolese of Monte Corona, for making these months of solitude available. They have been a time of extraordinary grace.

A special note of thanks to Father Charles for his joy and presence of God that were such a great encouragement during the time of solitude, and for his reading the handwritten draft and giving very helpful suggestions.

I want to extend a heartfelt thanks to the priests who were part of my life in the ministry and life of Bethany House of Intercession: Francis Bagan, O.M.I., George Beaune, C.S.B., Paul O'Brien, S.J., Gerald Farrell, M.M., Carl Hammer, James Henderson, O.C.S.O., Tod Laverty, O.F.M., Leo McCauley, S.J., Seraphim Michalenko, M.I.C., Archbishop George Pearce, S.M., Winus Roeten; and also to the priests I have shared my life and ministry with in the Fraternity of Priests: John Dreher, James Ferry, Edmund Sylvia, C.S.C., and Edward Wade; and those at the University of Steubenville, especially John Bertolucci and Michael Scanlan, T.O.R. and the priests at Holy Spirit Monastery.

One priest stands out among all the others, the one who had the greatest influence on my vocation and my spiritual growth and perseverance and that is my brother Bohdan Kosicki of the Archdiocese of Detroit, a classmate of Father Ed Scheuerman to whom these letters are addressed. May the Lord bless him with His infinite mercy.

Also I want to express my deepest appreciation and thanks to my religious community, the Basilian Fathers, and to the three successive Superior Generals who have assigned me to ministry to priests over these last sixteen years. It is through the vision and generosity of Father Joseph C. Wey, C.S.B., T. James Hanrahan, C.S.B., and Ulysse E. Pare, C.S.B., that I've been privileged to have the opportunity to minister to my brother priests.

A special thanks to Bishop Joseph McKinney, Auxiliary of Grand Rapids, Michigan, who encouraged me to begin and to continue spiritual ministry to my brother priests.

Finally, I want to extend my appreciation and special thanks to Sister Sophia Michalenko, C.M.G.T. for her most careful preparation of the manuscript and to Archbishop George Pearce, S.M. for his review of the draft text and constructive suggestions.

FOREWORD

Father George W. Kosicki, C.S.B.

Father Kosicki as director of the Department of Divine Mercy at the Congregation of Marians in Stockbridge, Massachusetts pursued a full-time apostolate of writing, preaching, and directing publications on the mercy of God. His roots with the Marians go quite deep. In the 1940's his family was introduced to the Marians—and the Divine Mercy devotion—through one of the Marian publications, "Rose Z Ogrodu Maryi" (Roses from the Garden of Mary).

When Father George entered the novitiate of the Basilian Fathers in 1946, his mother gave him a picture of the image of the Merciful Savior, which she had received from the Marians. It has hung in his room all these years, a daily reminder for him to trust in the mercy of God, and a continuous spiritual connection with the Marians.

Ordained in 1954, Father George obtained a doctorate in biochemistry in 1961 from the University of Michigan. After eleven years of teaching and experimental research in biochemistry, and five years of religious formation work, he was led to further pursue his growing interest in spiritual renewal, prayer life, and experimental work in community.

He became actively involved with the Charismatic Renewal movement and with Houses of Prayer in the Detroit area, and has given over one hundred retreats to priests in North, Central, and South America, Europe, and the Orient. From 1975-1983 he was coordinator of the Bethany House of Intercession, a community of priests, bishops, and deacons. From 1983-1986 he was a member of the Fraternity of Priests associated with the University of Steubenville in Ohio.

In addition to his twenty-four research publications in biochemistry, Father George has published numerous religious articles for such publications as *Review for Religious, Sisters Today, Crux, Emmanuel, Pastoral Life, The Crux of Prayer, New Covenant, Queen,* and *Homilitic and Pastoral Review.*

His published books include *The Promise: (the story of the film, Divine Mercy—No Escape), Like a Cedar of Lebanon, The Lord is My Shepherd, Forty-Days of Intercession, Key to the Good News, Rejoice in the Lord Always, The Good News of Suffering, Born of Mary, The Spirit and the Bride say, Come!* (with Father Gerald Farrell, M.M.), *Intercessory Prayer,* and the *Church in Travail in the 80's.*

1. SOMETHING MORE IS NEEDED!

October 10, 1985
Holy Family Hermitage

Dear Father Ed,

The Lord be with you in your time of sabbatical of renewal. I'm on sabbatical, too! I'm taking three months of solitude and silence with the Camaldolese Hermits to listen to the Lord. These past few years I've grown deaf and I haven't been able to hear the Lord and I've grown blind and I can't see what the Lord is doing. I just need the time to hear again and see clearly.

My heart has been heavy with the concern for the condition of the Church, especially for the condition of priests. You know my concern for priests over the years. We've shared often concerning their situation and the possible responses to their present needs.

Today? Something more is needed. And *more* is the key word. More is needed for the renewal of priests and I don't know what it is—although I suspect what it is. So, this sabbatical of solitude and silence is to listen to the Lord and to intercede for the church and especially bishops, priests, and deacons and then as a third possible priority to write on the priesthood.

Two Jesuit priests from Cleveland stopped by for a visit and in a short phrase they grasped why I was here at the hermitage. When I remarked that for fifteen years I had worked for the renewal of the priesthood by retreats, a house of intercession for priests, and by fraternity groups for support—but that much MORE was needed today, they spontaneously responded with an agreement, nodding their heads "Amen!"

Amen, Amen, more is needed. Renewal retreats, over a hundred of them on four continents were important and needed. So were eight years of Bethany House of Intercession, where some two thousand priests signed our guest book and where two out of three of them stayed with us to intercede for an extended time. The intercession for priests must continue but there is more needed. Over the past two years a team of four of us have worked out of the University of Steubenville setting up local fraternity groups of priests for mutual spiritual support. This is very important work but we are reaching less than 1% of the priests in the area where we work. For example, we recently held a four day conference aimed at setting up a local fraternity of priests in the Cleveland area. The local fraternity of five priests that was just beginning sent out invitations to 750 priests of the diocese but just one priest showed up. And he was contacted by a friend to come to this "special retreat." Something more than converting the 1% who do not need conversion is needed.

Ed, you know my love and concern for priests. We shared many priestly renewal programs together over the years: Vacations of rest and prayer in Quietico in 1954, the seven weeks of sharing and prayer at Washington, Michigan, 1970, seeking to renew our priestly lives and ministry, and our Pilgrimage to the Holy Land. You also interceded with us for priests at Bethany House of Intercession, Warwick, R.I., for thirty days in the summer of 1976. We shared many a day and long walks at the Pater Noster Club (R.&R. lodge for priests in the Detroit-Windsor Area located on Lake St. Clair) and over dinner or around the fireplace; I joined your weekly fraternity of brother priests many times and poured out my heart about priests and renewal. You know my work and love for priests but now I am searching for something more. Something more that the Lord wants for His priests.

This week you will be taking part in the first convocation of priests of the Archdiocese of Detroit. All the priests will be meeting for a week with the Archbishop. This is a good step but there is such a low morale and so much anger among these men! Something more is needed.

This November the bishops of the United States in their annual meeting in Washington, D.C., will be considering, among other things, the priest shortage and the even greater shortage of seminarians. At the peak in the sixties there were over 43,000 seminarians in the U.S.A. and now there are just over 10,000. The present situation is already difficult, but tomorrow's problem will be monumental. Something more is needed.

As you know, St. Martin's, your former parish, has no resident pastor. This situation is becoming more and more common. The priests are busy enough already, in fact, far too busy. Something more is needed.

So here I am at a hermitage, giving the Lord a blank check; "Fill it in, Lord!" I want to know and to do Your will. I no longer want to please men, but to please You. I am here to listen to You, Lord. Speak. I want to be available for what You want of me. Use me for the renewal of Your Church and Your priests. Something more is needed, Lord. You need to act in a sovereign way to renew us. Act now, Lord, in Your mercy and out of Your mercy.

Something more is needed, Lord, and that "something" is Your MERCY!

> In Jesus Our Lord
> and Mary our Mother,
> Fr. George

2. THE GRACE OF SOLITUDE

October 10, 1985
Holy Family Hermitage

Dear Father Ed,

The Lord be with you.

So here I am, in solitude and silence, listening to the Lord, praying and doing a bit of writing—as you see from this letter. Thanks to Father Charles the prior and Brothers Basil and Paul, I am served like a son of the King! I have a small hermitage cell—a little apartment with a study that has large picture windows on two sides, a small chapel with the Blessed Sacrament reserved, along with the icons of The Divine Mercy, Mother of Mercy and Jesus Crucified. Also, I have a bedroom with a solid, stiff bed and washroom. And outside there is an enclosed yard. There are nine such cells as mine clustered about the main chapel where Mass and the Divine Office are chanted. Meals are cooked by Fr. Charles and delivered to my cell—meals on wheels! Or is it Catering by Charles! A common building houses the kitchen, library, workshops, garage, laundry, and storage. The type of things lay brothers and servants used to do are now done by electricity and gas-powered motors.

My role here is to be in solitude and be present to the Lord. I celebrate the Eucharist daily with these men and preach a homily—sharing some of the current insights and graces. Besides that, I'm harvesting and shelling black walnuts. My black-stained fingers prove that very well!

I take time daily for a hike to the fields and meadows or forest which is located in a most picturesque hilly landscape in eastern Ohio. There are always more walnuts to pick up than I can possibly carry. It gives me good exercise physically, though, and it allows me just to be present to the Lord, rejoicing in His goodness and in His creation.

The main grace of the Holy Family Hermitage is the solitude. I spent two weeks here in August, by way of rest and discernment. I was so blessed by this time of grace that I sensed the Lord was calling me to three months of solitude. Permission came immediately and almost spontaneously. So here I am. In August it took me a week to slow down, quiet down and unwind until I was at peace. And then I could hear the Lord again. He speaks in such gentle whispers, like a gentle breeze. I was in such a whirlwind of traveling, talking, thinking and in internal darkness and turmoil that I could not hear the gentle word of the Lord. But when I became silent, then the gentle breeze was refreshing, and when the gentle breeze was recognized and responded to, it became a whirlwind of another sort! What a whirlwind of graces the Lord showered me with. I consider the main grace of the hermitage to be solitude. It is in solitude and silence that the Lord speaks with thunderclaps! I'll share some of these graces the best I can in future letters.

In the two weeks of hermitage during August, I asked Father Charles for material on the life of the Camaldolese Hermits. He gave me a series of books and documents. As I finished one, he gave me another. I devoured them. I read the life of Blessed Paul Giustiniani, the reformer of the Camaldolese and founder of the Camaldolese of Monte Corona, his rule, and some of his works and also some of the writings of St. Peter Damien, a Camaldolese and Doctor of the Church who recorded and developed the rule of the founder of the Camaldolese, St. Romuald. This style of hermitage is one that arose from St. Benedict who intended cenobitic life to be the school of Christian life. The monks that would be ready for more, for example, the apostolic life or the eremitical life. The eremitical dimension wasn't fully developed according to the intention of St. Benedict, until St. Romuald formed a community of hermits.

What impressed me about their lives and writings was the totalness of their dedication—all for God alone!—first and foremost. Then the other inspiring grace was solitude—so freely called "blessed solitude!" Not an escape from men and the world's needs but a flight to God Himself Who is the source of mercy and salvation for all. The scripture text that comes over and over again in their writings as central to this total response is:

> "I have been crucified with Christ; it is no longer I who live, but Christ who lives in me; and the life I now live in the flesh I live by faith in the Son of God, Who loved me and gave Himself for me." (*Gal.* 2:20)

St. Peter Damien in the book entitled *The Lord Be With You* wrote seven pages on solitude and the hermitage! He calls it: a school of heavenly learning, a paradise of delight, a warehouse of heavenly merchants, a workshop of spiritual labor, a tent of the holy army, God's fortress, an arena of spiritual warfare, a meeting place of God and man, the soul's purifying bath, the Lord's tomb, a spiritual dwelling place, the desert of Jesus. And I would add: a cenacle, the womb of Mary.

Yes, the grace of the hermitage is solitude and silence. To quote Father Jim Ferry in one of his pithy maxims: "The environment evangelizes." I have been evangelized to solitude and silence. I need it. I want it. I love it!

In Christ Jesus our Merciful Lord
and Mary our Mother,
Fr. George

3. NOW IS THE TIME FOR MERCY

October 11, 1985
Holy Family Hermitage

Dear Father Ed,

The Lord be with you!

Now is the time! The sense of timing of the Lord and awaiting the right time is alive in my thoughts and heart. What is the Lord's time for renewal of priests and the Church? I think it is a question of waiting on the Lord's timing with alertness for His anointing.

The Lord's anointing moves in waves or like the wind—it is here one moment and gone the next. So then waiting on the Lord, waiting with alertness in order to respond immediately is like surfing—you need to wait for the right moment to catch the big wave. Or it's like a glider that waits to catch the up-draft of the wind. Again, it is like the five wise virgins who waited with oil for their lamps, ready to meet the groom; or the disciples who waited in the upper room with Mary and with expectancy of the promise of the Lord for power to come upon them from on high.

So the renewal of priests is a question of waiting with alertness as much as it is a question of patience. The Lord has His rhythms and cycles. He created the days and nights, the seasons, growth and development.

Now is the time! I am coming to be more and more convinced that *now* is the time for *mercy!* All indications are pointing to a time of judgment by the Lord. And this present time before the judgment of the Lord is His time for mercy. Now is the time to plunge into the ocean of His mercy. But let me explain this sense of the coming judgment because it is crucial to our present timing and response.

Jesus is coming again—that is the faith we express when we pray the Credo and it is our prayer in every Eucharist and in every Our Father—"Thy kingdom come." Jesus will come again—that I know, but when and how He will come I don't know. However there are a number of persons who do know for sure when and even how He is coming—the Heavenly Father, Jesus our Lord, and the Holy Spirit and those to whom they have revealed something about it, namely, Mary our Mother as reported at Fatima and Medjugorje, and various saints and mystics, living and dead, for example, Sister Faustina, Padre Pio, Don Stefano Gobbi, and Teresa Musco, among others.

Currently I am reading once again the *Diary of Sister Faustina* which is truly a proclamation of God as The Divine Mercy, and reflecting on what that message means to priests. I would like to point out some of the reported revelations which Our Lord made to Sister Faustina of Cracow, Poland, during the 1930's and which deal with this topic of the coming of the Lord and the time of mercy. For example, here are a few entries in her diary:

> "Write down these words, My daughter. Speak to the world about My Mercy; let all mankind recognize My unfathomable mercy. It is the sign for the end of times; after it, will come the day of justice. While there is still time, let them have recourse to the fount of My mercy; let them profit from the Blood and Water which gushed forth for them" (II, 229 [848]).*

> "Secretary of My mercy, write, tell souls about this great mercy of Mine, because the awful day, the day of My justice, is near" (II, 305 [965]).

> "Before the Day of Justice I am sending the Day of Mercy" (V, 155 [1588]).

---

*The numbers given after quotations from Sister Faustina's Diary refer to the volume, page and paragraph as per the critical edition which is in Polish.

The Mother of God also appeared to Sister Faustina and said to her:

> "Oh, how pleasing to God is the soul that follows faithfully the inspirations of His grace! I gave the Savior to the world; as for you, you have to speak to the world about His great mercy and prepare the world for the Second Coming of Him who will come, not as a merciful Savior, but as a just Judge. Oh, how terrible is that day!"

> "Determined is the day of justice, the day of divine wrath. The angels tremble before it. Speak to souls about this great mercy *while it is still the time for [granting] mercy.* If you keep silent now, you will answer for a great number of souls on that terrible day. Fear nothing. Be faithful to the end. I feel for you" (II, 90 [635]) (Emphasis added).

Now is the day of mercy. Now is the time for seeking God's mercy. Now is the time for priests to preach and to teach all mankind and especially sinners and those in misery to turn to the Lord's mercy while it is still the time of mercy. The urgency is great and it is impressing itself upon me more and more. Souls are being lost because they are in sin and without mercy because they do not even know that there is such a thing as mercy. An ocean of mercy waits for those turning to the Lord and asking for mercy. We priests are the ones that need to be alerted first and then alert others—the time is short, the time is urgent, the time is now.

Our Lord is reported to have spoken to Sister Faustina about priests and their role:

> "I desire that *priests proclaim this great mercy of Mine* towards souls of sinners. Let the sinner not be afraid to approach Me. The flames of Mercy are burning Me—clamoring to be spent; I want to pour them out upon these souls" (I, 18 [50]) (Emphasis added).

This is the time of mercy. Now is the time for priests to preach and cry out to the ends of the world: "Come to the

mercy of the Lord while there is still time!"
Ed, I think that the "more needed" is *Mercy.*

> In Jesus, King of Mercy
> and in Mary, Mother of Mercy,
> Fr. George

4. THE FATHER OF MERCIES: THE MORE NEEDED IS MERCY

October 11, 1985
Holy Family Hermitage

Dear Father Ed,

I wrote to you that I think that "something more is needed" for renewal of priests, and that "Now is the time for mercy." From this solitude and time of waiting on the Lord I am equating the "need for more" with "Mercy". We priests need God's Mercy! We as priests need it first and foremost before we preach it to others. We need to know His mercy, experience it, be filled with it and TRUST the Lord as His sons and priests.

At this point, Ed, my mind is flying ahead and I want to relate three major graces of this sabbatical of solitude but I can only relate one at a time! Let me name them as: the *Father* as Giver of all good gifts, my being both the younger and elder son (described in the parable of the prodigal son) but *son* indeed, and my need for *trust* in the Lord. All these insights and graces are gifts of His Mercy. I'm torn between what to write on first! Maybe I should relate them in the sequence they are named because that is actually the order in which I experienced them. Let me tell you about them as personally and as simply as I can. Some of the graces you may resonate with and benefit by. Others may not apply directly to you but at least you'll appreciate and praise the Lord for them together with me.

So on to the grace of "The Father as Giver of all good gifts." (I'll tell you about the other two graces in further letters.)

October 14, 1985

During the second week of my two weeks of solitude in August, Father John Bertolucci, my pastoral leader (pastoral servant as he likes to call himself) came out to "serve" me. It really was a great service to me. He listened with an understanding heart to what has been going on over the past years, what made me so tired and drained and why I sought out a period of two weeks for solitude. I shared my deep desire for more solitude. He encouraged me to take three months of solitude and even volunteered to see Father Charles about the permission needed from the Camaldolese Superior General and also to write a memo to Father Michael Scanlan the overall pastoral leader of the Fraternity of Priests. Father John was a real father to me and opened up all the doors needed and here I am!

But John did more. He encouraged me, "Feel free to seek and follow the Father's will as a son" (referring to *Gal.* 4:7). He went on to say, "You have much to share in your writing that calls for silence, solitude, time—in a word, 'space' to do it."

In the Sacrament of Reconciliation that followed, John prayed and gave me the Scriptural text of *Galatians* 3:25 to 4:7, especially focusing on the fact that I am a son of the Father. I thanked him sincerely and he went on his way.

In prayer time afterwards I prayed, "Father, I ask You to know You and to know my sonship—as I know Mary as my Mother (Father John suggested this part of the prayer) and then I reflected on *Galatians* 3 and 4—I am son!

I was excited about the doors opening up for a time of silence and solitude. The next day, Father Charles phoned his Major Superior in Rome and received the clearance for my three month stay at Holy Family Hermitage!

Then the graces of Father as the Giver of all good gifts began to open up. As the first two weeks of hermitage were coming to a close I had the urging to review the journal entries, marking key points with red—and by writing a word or a phrase that summarized the point in the margin. It turned out that each entry was a key point! Each a gift and grace! So many graces and insights through these two weeks that I had to take two breaks from reviewing them because I thought I would "explode"— and I was only halfway into the review.

On the second break I went out toward a prayer spot—a pine knoll overlooking the hermitage. The sun had just broken through a heavy morning fog and on going out along the path, immediately a surprise met my eyes. Laced spider webs, magnificently constructed, glistening with a thousand minute water droplets—sparkling like diamonds. There were dozens of them on the spruce trees and on the fence, making the path a fairy land. I rejoiced and shouted in praise of the Father, the Giver of all good gifts. A few moments earlier, the sun would still be fogged in. A few moments later the droplets would have evaporated. Thank you, Father, for Your timing!

Then, on the way down from the pine knoll, a gentle breeze of a grace—a new love for priests!! What a gift, especially after experiencing a weakening in the ministry to priests these past few years. A new love for priests is such a special grace that I shall take time in another letter to share the meaning of it with you.

In Jesus our Lord
and Mary our Mother,
Fr. George

5. TRUST IN THE LORD

October 11, 1985
Holy Family Hermitage

Dear Father Ed,

And now about that insight and grace on "Trust in the Lord."

When I went to the novitiate to join the Basilian Fathers in August 1946, my mother gave me an icon of Jesus, The Divine Mercy, with the inscription in Polish "Jezu Ufam Tobie" (Jesus I Trust in You). It has hung in my room these many years and has been a focal point of prayer. Right now it is hanging in the little prayer chapel of this hermitage cell.

The other evening I asked the Lord to teach me about trust—a kind of request I used to make fairly frequently when I needed to know something about the Lord. He has been very faithful and prompt in responding. So I asked, "Lord, teach me what it means to trust You. I want to grow in trust of You. Help me, Mary." Then I went to bed and slept until I was awakened at midnight. I couldn't fall back asleep so I put on some warm clothes and went before the Lord before the Blessed Sacrament and then the fireworks started—insights into trust. I began to jot them down and more kept coming—some old insights I shared on retreats and forgot about, others new and mysterious, and some that will take more pondering and trusting. Then two and a half hours later I tried to sleep again but I couldn't. So I rested until 5:00 a.m. when I took time for more prayer and preparation for Mass.

I cannot convey the fireworks but at least I'll share the jottings. I sure didn't expect such a prompt and exciting answer to my request of the Lord!—nor at that time of the night! And so my jottings. To Trust means:

- ***To live out the "Our Father."*** As Jesus lived out His total trust in the Father so we are to trust. As Jesus was merciful as the Father, so we are to be merciful. With Jesus, and in Jesus, relying on Him, united with Him heart and mind we glorify the Father's name on earth as it is in Heaven, fulfilling His will to bring about His kingdom on earth as it is in Heaven, trusting Him for our daily bread and needs, forgiving those who offend us, and depending on Him to guard us and protect us from evil.

- ***To take His hand*** and walk in the light as a child, as a son, in simple faith. Thank God for the gesture of grasping His hand, and with the other hand, the hand of Mary. I find it a meaningful gesture, to walk hand in hand with Jesus and Mary.

    To ***rejoice*** always, ***pray*** without ceasing. In all things give ***thanks*** for this is the will of God for you all are in Christ Jesus. (Cf. *1 Thess.* 5:16-18, Confraternity Translation).

- ***To believe, to love, to hope in Jesus.***
    Trust is an umbrella word that takes in all three. It combines the past focus of faith in what Jesus did, the present, that is the "now" dimension of Christ's love, and the future dimension of hope because of what Jesus has prepared for us in Heaven.

    To ***be merciful***—like the Father and Jesus: in ***word*** to proclaim the Lord's mercy; in ***deed*** to do the will of the Father, serving and laying down our lives for the brethren; in ***prayer*** to glorify His mercy and implore His mercy on the whole world.

What does it mean to Trust?
It means to be totally absorbed in Jesus, to be "in love" with Him, to be present to Him, to seek Him, to rely on Him, to be possessed by Him, to be guided by Him, to believe in Him, to hope in Him, to love Him.

It means to have His mind and thoughts, His will, His plans, His timing, His power, His attitude, His heart—His Trust in the Father.

It means to live by the prayer "Jesus I trust in You!"
It means "It is no longer I that live by Christ!" (*Gal.* 2:20 RSV)
To Trust is to become You! It is no longer I that live but *You* (Cf. *Gal.* 2:20). It is to be divinized, to be transfigured by the Holy Spirit. This is the work of the Spirit.

The greatest work of the Holy Spirit was to *form Jesus!*—in the womb of Mary. His great work continues to be to *form Jesus in us,* that we be another "Jesus", born of Mary by the power of the Holy Spirit.

To trust Jesus is to invoke the Holy Spirit:—to implore Him: "Come! Holy Spirit, come and transform me, divinize me and transfigure me to be another Jesus."

To trust is to gaze on the Lord's glory with unveiled faces, and be transformed from glory, to glory, into His very image by the Lord who is the Spirit (see *2 Cor.* 3:18).

To trust is to **open** your eyes and see God, your ears and hear God, your mind and know God, your heart and love God, your arms and embrace God, your will and submit to God, your very self and to rely totally on Him.

Father of all mercies I Trust You! You are mercy Itself. Fill me with Your mercy that I may be merciful like Your beloved Son, Jesus. Fill me with Your mercy that I may be merciful like You. Fill me with Your mercy that I may be merciful to all and especially to sinners. Father of all mercies have mercy on all of us sinners. Father, fill me with Your mercy that I may be an apostle of mercy and radiate Your mercy.

After I finished these jottings, I went outside under the stars and cried out to God, "You're a crazy God!—to be so merciful!—to create me free that I might love You and trust You freely!—all at the terrible risk of my sinning and not trusting You. Lord, fill me with Your mercy that I may reflect Your mercy alone."

Ed, this is a glimpse of the "midnight grace." It can be exciting and at times very surprising to ask the Lord to teach you—especially about Trust.

Trusting in the Lord,
Fr. George

6. MORE TRUST

October 12, 1985
Holy Family Hermitage

Dear Father Ed,

Since the letter on the "midnight grace" and the meaning of trust, more awareness of trust has come from a variety of sources. I was sharing with Father Charles about the need of prayer for a priest that I know who had just this week received a prison sentence of fifteen years (twelve of them suspended, thank God) for pedophilia. "Lord, have mercy on my brother." Father Charles responded, "We need to give him over to the mercy of God and *TRUST* that God will care for him in his great mercy. It takes real trust in God, like Abraham who put his trust in God and then walked in that trust. It takes trust to place this priest in God's mercy and then not be overcome with sadness." Like the psalmist says, "Put your Trust in God and He will do it."

I kept in mind what Father Charles said about trusting as I prayed for this priest. I also wrote to him encouraging him, "Trust and offer your sufferings, no matter what the origin, in union with the Eucharistic Lord for salvation of souls. Your sufferings are very precious and bring salvation to souls when offered in love with Christ's suffering. Christ sanctified suffering by His love and now has invited you to suffer with Him." This takes real trust when you're behind prison bars for three years.

I also reflected on what Father Charles said and looked up the section on Abraham in Genesis and other texts of Scripture as well, that speak of radical Trust in the Lord.

Abram was given a great promise of many descendants by the Lord when he was old and had no son and Sarah his wife was beyond the age of child bearing—yet "Abram put his faith in the Lord, who credited it to him as an act of righteousness" (*Gen.* 15:6). Abram trusted when all human conditions would make the promise impossible. Yet by God's mercy, Abram with his new name of Abraham, promising him to be the father of many nations, at one hundred years old fathered his son Isaac by his wife Sarah. Abraham trusted God and God acted.

The psalm sings of this radical trust in the Lord:

> "If you **trust in the Lord and do good,** then you will live in the Lord and be secure. If you find your delight in the Lord, He will grant you your heart's desire. **Commit your lives to the Lord, trust in Him and He will act,** so that your justice breaks forth like the light, your cause like the noon-day sun. **Be still before the Lord** and wait in patience..." (*Ps.* 35)

"Trust in Him and He will act," He will do it. Only "Be still before the Lord"—don't lose your cool—don't let sadness overwhelm you. This speaks to me.

In writing about Abraham, St. Paul says that:

> "All depends on faith, everything is grace," (*Rom.* 4:16) and about the gospel, "For in the gospel is revealed the justice of God which begins with faith": as Scripture says, "The just man shall live by faith" (*Rom.* 1:17).

St. Paul is writing about a radical trust in God.

Mary, like Abraham, trusted when the human condition was impossible, "How can this be since I do not know man?" (*Lk.* 1:34). When the angel explained that the Holy Spirit would come upon her, Mary responded with the great act of faith, "I am the servant of the Lord. Let it be done to me as you say" (*Lk.* 1:38).

Jesus called for this kind of radical trust from His disciples, for example, when He responded to Martha's concern about the death of her brother Lazarus:

I am the Resurrection and the Life. Whoever believes in Me, though he should die, will come to life; and whoever is alive and believes in Me will never die. ***Do you believe this?*** "Yes, Lord," she replied. "I have come to believe that You are the Messiah, the Son of God; He Who is to come into the world" (*Jn.* 11:26-27).

Jesus Himself, like Abraham and like Mary His Mother, trusted when all human conditions were impossible. Crying out His dying words on the cross, He entrusted Himself to the Father, "Father, into Your hands I commend My spirit" (*Lk.* 23:46), knowing that the Father would raise Him from the dead. This is radical trust!

And what about a priest now in prison for three years? How can he trust? He has already repented to God. He chose the way of no contention in the court, putting himself at the mercy of the judge because he did not want the young boys to be publicly embarrassed by the court review, and by the sensationalism of the newspaper reporting. He can now trust by entrusting himself to the Lord, and offering his suffering in atonement for his own sins and those of the whole world. He can trust that his suffering, offered with love, is salvific.

How can I trust in his regard? I woke up out of a fitful sleep last night with him on my heart and mind. What can I do? I battled off my spirit of sadness and fretting that could easily lead me into depression. I renounced those spirits in the name of Jesus, bound them and sent them to Jesus. I sprinkled the cell with holy water and went before the Blessed Sacrament and commended my priest friend to the mercy of God.

Yes, I can do something for my brother priest. I can entrust him to the mercy of God with a simple act of the will and keep him immersed in the infinite ocean of God's mercy. It is a simple act of intercession, but a radical act of trust in the Lord—that He will act with mercy in his regard and accept his offering of suffering. Also, I can entrust to the Lord the boys involved and their parents, the judges and lawyers and the bishop of the diocese, all those in some way connected with this case and immerse them in the mercy of God.

Jesus is reported to have complained to Sister Faustina in these words,

"Distrust on the part of souls is tearing at My insides. The distrust of a chosen soul causes Me even greater pain; despite My inexhaustible love for them they do not trust Me. Even My death is not enough for them. Woe to the soul that abuses these gifts." [I, 18]

Commit your lives to the Lord, Trust in Him and He will act (*Ps.* 35).

Jesus I Trust in You!
Fr. George

7. A NEW LOVE FOR PRIESTS

October 16, 1985
Holy Family Hermitage

Dear Father Ed,

One day during the first two weeks of solitude as I was coming down from the prayer spot, the pine knoll overlooking the hermitage, I sensed that, like a gentle breeze, God was giving me a special grace: a new love for priests. It was such a very gentle breeze that I wondered if it were indeed the Lord's grace. If it was the Lord, then I knew that it would grow into a whirlwind.

I welcomed this grace, this new love for priests, because over these past two years I felt a growing inadequacy in ministering to priests along with an increasing distaste for this type of ministry. The new love was a desire to call priests to be who they are—victims with Christ, warriors with Christ, yet little in the arms of Mary. They, like the bread of the Eucharist, are called, blessed (ordained), and broken to be given. Priests are to be Eucharist. They are to be Mercy Incarnate like Jesus Himself.

I wrote out a prayer of thanks to Mary for this grace and asked her to help us priests to be priests after the Eucharistic Heart of Jesus.

What does this new love mean? The Lord will open up the meaning and open up the doors needed. At present my "romping in the vision" brought out these aspects:

- a call for more *intercession* for priests to "move on" to the fullness of their priesthood,
- a clearer call to *write* on the priest as victim, as a man of mercy and of the Eucharist,

- a growing desire for a **house** for priests to grow in this dimension of their priesthood,
- a call to **challenge** priests to become **warriors** for Church, to become victims in and with Christ, to become the priests they are ordained to be, yet like little children in the arms and in the heart of Mary,
- a call to **challenge** priests to **go all the way**—all for God! I'm inspired by so many of the priest-saints, whose sanctity consisted not in great deeds but, through God's grace, in simplicity, humility, purity and mercy.

It would be living out the priesthood as envisaged by mystics in our time: Conchita of Mexico, Sister Faustina of Cracow, Don Stefano Gobbi of Milan, Padre Pio of Pietrelcina.

After this reflection I took a hike beyond the woods, through the cornfields to a cattle gate I saw a way off. It opened to an idyllic pasture, and I thought that I had suddenly stepped into a pastoral scene in Ireland or England. At the lower level of pasture a clear stream with hundreds of little fish divided the green meadow! On the side of the meadow the largest oak tree I've ever seen reigned over the scene. I picked some wild mint leaves for tea and a quart of chokecherries for jelly. All of this a gift from the Father, Giver of all gifts.

I heard this word within me, "This for My son whom I love. All the graces of these past two weeks have been a gift! The new love for priests is My gift to you My son!" I looked at the Scriptures on the altar: . . . how much more will your heavenly Father give good things to anyone who asks Him! (*Matt.* 7:11).

As I reflected on this passage, it seemed to me that the Lord was saying: "George, tell my priests that they are My sons; that they are priests and victims with Jesus My Beloved Son."

I'll end with this entry which concluded my written evaluation of the two weeks: "I've grown a beard as a visible sign and reminder that I need silence and solitude to listen to the Lord." Now after two months, I'm not sure if I look like an old sea captain or a monk.

May the Father reveal His gifts to you,
Fr. George

8. UNITY OF BISHOP AND PRIESTS

October 17, 1985
Holy Family Hermitage

Dear Father Ed,

Today is the feast of St. Ignatius of Antioch, a great lover of the Lord Jesus and a great lover of the Church. I read through his seven letters to the various Churches located along his route to martyrdom in Rome, and became aware of how important he considered unity with the bishop. It seems that he considered it a true mark of Christianity. In each of the letters he speaks of this unity, for example:

> "Just as the Lord, being one with the Father, did nothing, either in His person or through the Apostles, without the Father, so you should do nothing without the bishop and the council of priests. Nor should you try to make a thing out to be reasonable merely because it seems so to you personally; but let there be in common a single prayer, one petition, one mind, one hope, in love, in the unmixed joy which is Jesus Christ, who is the best of all. Hasten all of you together as to one temple of God, to one altar, to Jesus Christ alone, who came forth from one Father in whom He is and to whom He has returned" (St. Ignatius, *to the Magnesians*).

Here he is writing of the unity of all the Christians, that they may be one, after the prayer of Jesus (see *Jn.* 17:21). But Ignatius gets more specific and also addresses the priests:

> "Hence it is right for you to concur, as you do, with the mind of the bishop. For you priests, who are worthy of the name and worthy of God, like the strings of a lyre, are in harmony with the bishop. Hence it is that in the harmony of your minds and hearts Jesus Christ is hymned. Make of yourselves a choir, so that with one voice and one mind, taking the key note of God, you may sing in unison with one voice through Jesus Christ to the Father, and He may hear you and recognize you, in your good works, as members of His Son. It is good for you, therefore, to be in perfect unity that you may at all times be partakers of God" (St. Ignatius, *to the Ephesians*).

Let me lament for a while! Lord, when will this ever happen! Your Son Jesus prayed for such unity at the Last Supper: "That they all may be one as You, Father, are in Me and I in You; I pray that they may be one in Us, that the world may believe that You sent Me" (*Jn.* 17:21). Lord, how will the world believe unless the prayer of Your Son Jesus is answered. When will we priests be one in heart and one in mind with our bishops!? When will we sing one melody like strings on a harp? Lord, I know that You've heard the prayer of Your Son for unity, so I ask You to help us to become part of the answer. Even Your own Son Jesus, following the very supper at which He prayed for this kind of unity for His disciples, experienced the betrayal of Judas, the denial of Peter and the desertion of the other apostles. How precious this unity, if it comes with such a price, the death of Your Son.

And yet there are sparks of this unity among the bishops and their priests. I've seen it and experienced it on a few occasions. But how can most bishops and priests be made aware of the essential need of this unity. I leave you to answer this question: "What was your experience of the convocation of the Archbishops and all the priests of the Archdiocese of Detroit, this past week?"

It certainly is the desire of the Second Vatican Council that bishops and priests form a united presbyterate:

> "Priests, prudent cooperators with the episcopal order as well as its aids and instruments, are called

to serve the people of God. They constitute one priesthood with their bishop, although that priesthood is comprised of different functions... On account of this sharing in his priesthood and mission, let priests sincerely look upon their bishop as their father, and reverently obey him. And let the bishop regard his priests, who are his co-workers, as sons and friends, just as Christ called His disciples no longer servants but friends" (Cf. *Jn.* 15:15). ("Lumen Gentium," #28)

There are many similar statements in the Decree on the Ministry and Life of Priests, e.g., #7 and 8—but how do these documents and decrees get transferred from paper into reality? It is all very nice on paper but where is it happening?

When we were starting to promote local priest fraternity groups two years ago, a priest in West Virginia made a very perceptive observation about our attempts. "In trying to gather the priests together in order to support each other and help renew one another, you are doing the work of the bishop. This is what the bishop should be doing, not you!" This observation has remained with me, especially as I see the minimal response we are getting as we go directly to priests.

Really, what is a priest without his bishop? A nothing and a nobody. And what is a bishop without his priests? A man with amputated arms and legs. The local presbyterate is one body.

Don't think that I have the answer! That's why I'm here in this hermitage, seeking, waiting, listening. I do know, though, that the Lord wants the prayer of His Son Jesus be answered, "That they all be one." So my present response to the lack of unity of bishops and their priests is to continue to intercede: "Father, that we may be one. Hear the prayer of Your Son, Jesus. Father, look upon the broken Body of Your Son and have mercy."

On this feast of St. Ignatius of Antioch there is a step that all of us priests can take toward that unity; and that is to encourage our bishops in prayer, words, letters and deeds when we see the Spirit of God at work. In the words of St. Ignatius:

> "All of you without exception, and ***particularly the priests,*** must help to keep up the bishop's spirit

out of reverence for the Father and Jesus Christ and the Apostles" (*to the Trallians*).

We can be like Aaron and Hur supporting the tired arms of Moses in the battle against Amalek. As long as Moses' arms were held up high, the Israelites had the better of the fight (*Ex.* 17:8-13). The bishop is our father and needs our cooperation and help.

The other example of St. Ignatius is that we too become wheat ground for the bread of Christ (see *to the Romans*). Unity is purchased at a great price—all that we have.

In the unity of Christ Jesus,
Fr. George

9. THE GRACE OF SONSHIP: TAKE MY HAND...

October 18, 1985
Holy Family Hermitage

Dear Father Ed,

A very special grace of God's mercy began to open up on the feast of St. Thérèse of Lisieux. I was reading her life by J.B. Morton in a collection of lives of the saints called *Saints and Ourselves,* (Servant Books, Ann Arbor, MI 48107), and a sentence quoting St. Thérèse struck me: "It is for us to console Our Lord, not for Him to be always consoling us." And again, when from Communion she received no consolation: "Is not this to be expected, since I do not desire to receive our Lord for my own satisfaction, but to please Him?"

"To console our Lord...To please Him" stayed with me. These words reminded me of the mystical phrase of Pope John Paul II, having mercy on the Son of God: "In a special way, God also reveals His mercy when He invites man to have mercy on His only Son, the Crucified one." ("Dives in Misericordia," #8)

These phrases and the concept of pleasing God rather than pleasing men kept growing in my consciousness. In prayer I became aware of how much I sought to please myself or others, rather than the Lord. It became a real conviction. I'm a pleaser of man, not of God! I looked up and wrote out those penetrating words of Jesus in the Gospel of John:

> "I say only what the Father taught Me. The One who sent Me is with Me. He has not deserted Me since I always do what pleases Him (*Jn.* 8:28b-29)

...I tell you what I have seen in the Father's presence (*Jn.* 8:38). How can people like you believe, when you accept praise from one another yet do not seek the glory that comes from the one God (*Jn.* 5:44). They preferred the praises of men to the glory of God" (*Jn.* 12:43).

I became more and more aware of how fearful I was of what other people thought or might think. I'm a people pleaser! This phrase was given to me as the reason so many of us priests and bishops do not speak out when we see something wrong or someone in error. I was at a national meeting during the time when a supposed Catholic theologian was publicly teaching a pro-abortion stance. I asked one of the guest speakers privately, a professor of spirituality at the Gregorian University in Rome, "Why doesn't the local bishop do something about this theologian?" He answered that bishops, like we priests, are people pleasers!

I began praying for a healing in this area of fear of what other people think. I realized that it was a fear that paralyzed me in my freedom to act as a son of the Father.

The first response was an insight that brought together many facets of concern to me: It is a sin to try to please others rather than God; the truth is that I do not trust God Who is present, Who is my Father and Whose son I am; I am free but I need to know it; I feel more like a prisoner of my fears of others' opinion and get intimidated easily.

The next step was a crystallization of this awareness in the analysis of the elder son, in the parable of the prodigal son. The elder son on the surface had no need of conversion of life and no need of his father's mercy, but he had a bad relationship with his father, brother, and even with his friends. He had a false idea of perfection. He was a prisoner obsessed with perfectionism, in pleasing self, suppressing every fault, preoccupied with not displeasing the other, full of fears. By an inversion the fear of God's negative judgment derives from the desire to be accepted by God and so he tries to correct all imperfections!—Tries to "buy" God's benevolence—does not trust Him! Faith is transformed into a search for a guarantee of benevolence. Legalism hides unbelief.

"My son, you are with me always, and everything I have is yours" (*Lk.* 15:31). Thus the elder son does not really know the father; he needs to discover and welcome the presence of the one who is a benevolent father! Then the resolution applies it to the heavenly Father. Faith in divine Fatherhood frees!...because the believer knows that God's benevolence is stronger than our human weakness. *Faith* shifts attention from self to God, accepts our frailty and so confesses sin. *Humility* recognizes the truth regarding self and God—"it confers a certain serenity and optimistic goodness." *Brotherhood* is a consequence of the experience of Fatherhood, recognizing "Traces of the Father's goodness in self and others with joy!" All this is in opposition to the elder son's irritation at the Father's goodness which was a *threat* to his self-perfection, and his idea of God and a perceived *disapproval* of his legalism, by withholding approval. So he seeks his own perfection by action, production, and demonstration of self-worth.

After that analysis of the elder son I felt like both, the younger prodigal son and the elder son! Neither of them knew the Father. Isn't this true of so many of us priests—we try to be faithful and good by our own efforts. Are we trying to prove something or merit something? Are we trying to please someone? Are we really trying to please God? I have shared this analysis because I thought that you also could make use of it in ministering to priests.

But there is more to this story—the resolution is seen but the healing is yet to come. I thanked the Father for the converging insight that: "I am a son of the Merciful Father, and this by His mercy. I am also a sinner but His mercy is greater than my sin—my self-perfection, my pride, my fears of others' opinions." Then I asked for purification and healing: "Lord, I'm both the younger and the elder son. I need conversion and mercy. Purify me and heal me. Mary, teach me to trust in Jesus and have the freedom and power of a son of the Father."

I experienced the mercy and care of the loving Father immediately, in a very practical way. I wanted to gather black walnuts from the meadows and pasture right next door but I was fretting about asking and getting permission of a neighboring farmer to gather nuts from his farm. Just as I started to walk towards his farm, he came down the road and joyfully invited me to pick all I wanted, even to pick up the nuts from the tree in his backyard! It turns out that he leases the beautiful upper cornfield and part of the meadow from Father

Charles. On that trip I returned with a bushel of nuts. These have started me on my project of husking, cracking, shelling and drying bushels of black walnuts. It's my daily "recreation." The loving Father provides for all and showed me I had no need for "fears."

As the days went by, I continued to pray for purification and healing. I became increasingly conscious of how many fears of others and others' opinions there were within me. Are my fears of being criticized and of rejection and of non-affirmation, all projected onto the heavenly Father? Lord, where is the balance between charity, service and true concern for others on the one hand, and trying not to displease others out of a fear of non-acceptance and fear of criticism? Lord, I see the fears in me in regard to others. I can make a litany of them, but I'm blind and deaf when it comes to being aware of fears of You; fears that rob me of the freedom and power I should have as a son of God. Show me, Lord, the obstacles to trust in You! As I offered this prayer to God, a list of these fears came to me so I jotted them down: irritations, impatience, judgmentalism, anger with others' ways, timing, mannerisms, and theological positions different from my own; and then, fears of future calamities, fears of false piety, fears of displeasing the Lord, and being anxious about details and arrangements; and especially my not rejoicing, not praying, not thanking the Lord always and everywhere.

Then came the purifying and the healing—the resolution to the fears and obstacles to trusting Him. In a way that makes me laugh, the Lord once again used the exhortation He used so many times over the years, beginning with the Thirty-Day directed spiritual exercises of St. Ignatius of Loyola, back in January of 1974. But this time it came with fuller meaning and with healing:

- ***Take My hand***—grasp it! Trust, accept My presence, My love, My guidance, My protection, and with the other hand take Mary's hand!
- ***and walk***—with Me, not ahead or behind Me. Walk, not run, nor stand still. Walk patiently in My timing and pace. Come with Me, under My yoke together with Me.
- ***as a child, as a son***—a little child, docile, simple, flexible, loving, and lovable, blessed, embraced by

Me, a child of the heavenly Father, a child of Mary our Mother, My little brother whom I so love. Be little, be loved, be lovable—be a son!
- ***in simple faith***—TRUST ME. Trust My Father and yours. I am the Lord of Heaven and earth—all is under My dominion—TRUST ME. Let Me love you and embrace you, bless you and care for you. Have faith in Me—trust in Me is the source of freedom and power.

[With sobs and healing tears in my eyes I reach out and grasp your hands, Jesus and Mary. Take me to the Father—mine and yours.]

- ***Walk in the Light***—in the truth, profess it, live it, do not be afraid of seeing error and darkness. I need you to be strong—by being a little child. I take you into My arms and bless you and reveal the light of My presence. I need you strong but little.
- ***So, Rejoice Always***—you are son of the Father, of Mary, like I am! Praise the Father.
- ***Thank always and everywhere***—For He is good and merciful and the Giver of all good gifts, He is benevolent! He loves you so, and cares for you so! You are His beloved son. Thank Him and rejoice.
- ***Pray always***—ASK—INTERCEDE in, with, and through Me. This is your special charism. You are priest in and with and through Me, the one Intercessor. Let us together, with Mary and the Saints plead for mercy on the whole world.

This grace of insight into the merciful Father and the elder son is a grace for a whole life. A healing of fears has already taken place and I rejoice in it. Certainly the Lord will continue His purifying and healing, but the grace and healing already received is a challenge and nourishment for a lifetime!

The grace of "grasping the hand of Jesus" with an actual gesture is a precious gift not only for me but for many of my brother priests. They, too, can "Take My hand and walk in the light as a child, as a Son, in simple faith and 'Rejoice always, pray without ceasing, in all things give thanks, for

this is the will of God in Christ Jesus regarding you all' "
(*1 Thess.* 5:16-18, Confraternity Translation).

I've shared this personal insight and healing grace because I realize so many of us priests need to know and experience such a grace—to heal us of our fears and obstacles, no matter what they may be. He wants us to turn to His infinite mercy, receive it and to know and experience that God is our Father and that we are His sons.

Jesus, I Trust in You,
Fr. George

10. APOSTLES OF MERCY

October 19, 1985
Holy Family Hermitage

Dear Father Ed,

The Lord of mercies be with you.

In the letter on "The Grace of Sonship: Take My hand..." I described a purification and a healing that then moved into a prayer of asking to be an "apostle of mercy."

The awareness of the need to proclaim God's mercy has been growing within me during these days of solitude at the hermitage. I've been preaching each morning at the community Eucharist and generally the message centers on God's mercy. Father Charles keeps telling me that God is calling me to be an apostle of mercy—he says power flows when I proclaim His mercy, His infinite loving kindness for us. Also, I've been doing work on the *Diary of Sr. Faustina,* preparing for priests a little booklet that would relate the words of our Lord and of Sister Faustina on Mercy that are directly addressed to priests.

I am growing in the conviction that all of us priests are to be ministers of mercy to our people and to the world. But the work of mercy has to begin within—within me—before I can reach out with mercy to others. I need to be as merciful as my Father is merciful! (see *Lk.* 6:36). I can't give what I haven't got! And so I ask:

> Father, fill me with Your mercy that I may be merciful.
>
> Father, I ask for mercy not only for myself but for all Your bishops, all Your priests and deacons.
>
> Father, *fill us* with Your mercy that we may be merciful.

Make us ***icons*** of Your mercy that others may see Your mercy and be drawn into Your mercy.

Make us ***instruments*** of Your mercy to open up others to Your mercy, to prepare for Your coming.

Make us ***intercessors*** of Your mercy, imploring Your mercy on us and on the whole world.

Make us ***vessels*** of Your mercy to bring mercy to others that they may experience Your mercy.

Make us ***preachers*** of Your mercy to tell others of Your mercy that they may hear of Your mercy and be converted.

Make us ***teachers*** of Your mercy to explain and take away obstacles to receiving Your mercy.

Make us ***writers*** of Your mercy that many may read of Your mercy and open their hearts to you.

Make us ***apostles*** of Your mercy, sent by You to proclaim Your kingdom of mercy, Your time of mercy, Your plan of mercy.

Lord, fill us with Your mercy that we may be as merciful as You are merciful.

To be "apostles of mercy" would mean a radical and total trust in the Lord Jesus Who reveals the mercy of the Father to us. So the battle cry of an apostle of mercy is: "JESUS, I TRUST IN YOU!" This act of trust can be a summary of the gospel and our response to it. In a sense, "it says it all!"

"Jesus, I Trust in You" is the act of trust Jesus asked Sister Faustina to have inscribed on His image as The Divine Mercy. "Jesus, I Trust in You" is the prayer we live by as Apostles of Mercy.

Last week I read in "Our Lady speaks to Her Beloved Priests" (November 27, 1973): "I will grant all their requests and satisfy their deepest desires!" I thought to myself—what is my deepest desire? What is the greatest desire of my heart?

- to proclaim Jesus Incarnate Mercy and Mary the Mother of Mercy,
- to proclaim the mystery of mercy and Mary publicly, by every means possible, and

- to live out of a supportive community of intercession, solitude and silence;
- in a word, to be an apostle of mercy
- to prepare priests and people NOW for the coming of the Lord.

So this is what I see that Priests need—mercy—and trust in that Infinite, Divine Mercy.

In the Mercy of the Lord,
Fr. George

P.S. Yesterday was the feast of St. Luke—a patron of mercy and one of the great apostles of mercy. His gospel brings out God's mercy in a clear and inspiring way. He portrays Jesus bringing God's covenant of mercy to the poor, the weak, the sinners, and the needy. He relates the great parables of mercy: The Lost Sheep, The Lost Coin, The Prodigal Son, The Good Samaritan, The Pharisee and the Publican at prayer. He recalls the merciful deeds of Jesus: healing, delivering and forgiving. He shows the compassion of Jesus toward women, and relates Mary's role in the merciful incarnation. But more than that, St. Luke portrays and participates in the great proclamation and outpouring of God's mercy throughout the then known world as recorded in the Acts of the Apostles.

11. MARTYRDOM

October 19, 1985
Holy Family Hermitage

Dear Father Ed,

Today is the feast of Sts. John de Brebeuf, Isaac Jogues and companions—Martyrs. What about martyrdom? Is that in store for us today?

Listen to St. John de Brebeuf, priest and martyr: "For two days now I have experienced a great desire to be a martyr and to endure all the torments the martyrs suffered" (The Jesuit Relations, Liturgy of the Hours for October 19). Then he goes on to make a vow to God "never to fail to accept the grace of martyrdom, if some day You in Your infinite mercy should offer it to me, Your most unworthy servant."

I've been told by various people that in this our day we have more martyrs than in the early days of the Church under the persecutions from the Roman Empire. Also, a number of present-day mystics tell of a coming time of persecution, especially of priests. What can we expect? What are we to do about it?

In 1975, during our intercessory month for priests in Rome, Italy, forty of us priests made a day's pilgrimage to the shrines of the martyrs. We prayed at the tomb of St. Peter in the lower level of St. Peter's Basilica, we prayed at the tomb of St. Paul, then went on to the Quo Vadis Church and then to the Catacombs of St. Callistus where we concelebrated mass at the altar of martyrdom of St. Sebastian. During the assembly, one of the priests spoke out prophetically, "I am calling you to martyrdom, some of you here will be martyrs." A number of priests had the same sense—the word stayed with me as we returned to Bethany House of Intercession in Rhode Island. We asked ourselves the meaning of this word. "If it is true, then how do we prepare for martyrdom?" Father Jim Henderson, the Trappist with us from New Melleray Abbey in Iowa, answered with the simple phrase: "By dying daily!"

That's it! We can do something about martyrdom. We can prepare for it! We can die daily. You and I know how many ways we can "die" each day. "Whoever wishes to be My follower must deny his very self, take up his cross each day, and follow in My footsteps" (*Lk.* 9:23)—I must die daily!

We too must be "foolish" like St. Thomas and say to our fellow disciples, "Let us go along and die with Him" (*Jn.* 11:16). We too will need to drink the cup that He was to drink (see *Matt.* 20:23). "It is for this you were called, since Christ suffered for you in just this way and left an example, to have you follow in His footsteps" (*1 Ptr.* 2:21). "All this is as God intends, for it is your special privilege to take Christ's part—not only to believe in Him but also to suffer for Him" (*Phil.* 1:28b-29).

I sense that moving in the direction of an apostolate of mercy, with an urgency of preparing for the Lord's coming in the near future, is an excellent way to prepare for and also to ask for martyrdom.

> In the mercy of our Lord Jesus,
> Fr. George

12. MARY, MOTHER OF GOD AND MY MOTHER

October 21, 1985
Holy Family Hermitage

Dear Father Ed,

Praised be the Lord Jesus Christ, Son of the Father and Son of Mary!

Mary continues to be very present in this time of solitude. Mary is so central to my life and priesthood that I want to write a letter to honor her and so encourage all priests to come to a closer relationship with the Mother of God. In this letter I want to review the basic reasons and need for our devotion to Mary and share with you my own devotion.

The central grace and role of Mary is that she is the Godbearer, the Theotokos, the Mother of God. I honor our Orthodox brethren for being so faithful and clear in this truth of our faith. Their devotion to the Mother of God in the Divine Liturgy, the Office of Praise of the Mother of God (Acathist Hymn), and in their icons has inspired me to pray the Acathist Hymn on Mary's feast days and to pray daily before her icon, Our Lady of Mercy (of the tenderness series). This icon portrays and presents the central grace and revelation of the Incarnation. Jesus Christ, true God and true man, is Son of the Father and Son of Mary, born of Mary by the power of the Holy Spirit. As I stand before this icon I am drawn into this grace and into the embrace of Jesus and Mary. Jesus embraces simultaneously all of humanity, the Church, His mother and me. This icon is for me a theology of incarnation in image.

Mary's virginal Motherhood was explicitly extended to all

mankind (see John Paul II, "Redemptor Hominis," #22) when in His dying words on the cross, Jesus said to His mother, "Woman, behold your son!" (*Jn.* 19:26).

Mary is not only Mother of God but she is also Mother of all mankind. Because of God's choice and appointment, her central role is to be "Mother." She is Mother to each and every one of us, so that she can do for us what she did for Jesus, form us into Jesus by the power of the Holy Spirit. Her great work is to form Jesus. So, too, it is the great work of the Holy Spirit to form Jesus. Mary and the Spirit united give us Jesus. I first realized this and preached it in 1983 at the All Michigan Conference in East Lansing, Michigan, held at the Michigan State University (M.S.U.) so the slogan of the conference became "M.S.U."—"Mary, Spirit, United give us Jesus!" The green and white letters were posted everywhere so it wasn't hard to remember the point of the talk! M.S.U.!

At one time I had a difficulty in my relationship with Mary, as there were hesitancies and questions that were obstacles to this close embrace and to entrusting my life to her in a deeper consecration. But, thanks be to God, in a moment of grace these obstacles were removed while I was attending the funeral of a priest friend, Father Mike Hiegel, M.M., a Maryknoll missioner in the Philippines for over twenty years. Father Mike had a great love of Mary. In fact this grace began for me many years earlier when I was giving retreats in the Philippines and got to know this great Marian missionary and then and then again when he came to us in a wheelchair to Bethany House for two months to intercede for priests. Shortly afterwards he died of complications from his sickness. While waiting for the funeral mass which was at Maryknoll, N.Y., I read an essay by Cardinal Suenens, "Who Is She?" in *Essays on Renewal,* (Servant Books, Ann Arbor, MI 48107) and was touched by two things that the Cardinal said—I received them as graces obtained through the intercession of Father Mike.

One grace was that the concern I had about deciding about a deeper consecration to Mary was taken away. Cardinal Suenens said something to the effect, "I don't need to decide to choose Mary, that's already done! God did that a long time ago! I only need to receive her!" I then realized that I don't need to be anxious about whether or not to choose Mary, to embrace Mary, to entrust myself to Mary—all I need to do is to do it! So I did!

And the other grace from the same essay came from what Cardinal Suenens said about the message of the Lord to St. Joseph about Mary, when St. Joseph was worried about what to do with Mary. The Cardinal said that what the angel said to Joseph, the Lord says to each of us: "Do not be afraid to take Mary to yourself because what is in her is of the Holy Spirit!" All fear disappeared in me. How could I hesitate any longer? So I didn't. I consecrated myself anew and in a deeper way.

Consecration to Mary is a way of allowing Mary to be mother to me. It is allowing her to form me into the living icon of Jesus. It is entrusting my consecrated life into her motherly care so she can do for me what she did for Jesus—namely, form Him and then teach Him as mother, docility, obedience and love of the Father. It is allowing both Mary and myself to fulfill the dying command of Jesus on the cross: "Woman, behold, your son!" and "Son, behold, your mother!" (*Jn.* 19:26-27). It is taking Mary as my own, as my inheritance, taking into the deepest part of my being that the Word may be made flesh in me.

Taking Mary as my Mother, taking her as my own, is expressed in various ways in my life. I have led many priests and people in their consecration or renewal of their consecration to Mary using this prayer:

An Act of Consecration to Mary

Mary, Mother of Jesus
    and Mother of Mercy,
    since Jesus from the Cross
    gave you to me,
    I take you as my own.
And since Jesus gave me to you,
    take me as your own.
Make me docile
    like Jesus on the Cross,
    obedient to the Father,
    trusting in humility and love.
Mary, my Mother,
    in imitation of the Father,
    who gave His Son to you,

> I too give my all to you;
> to you I entrust all that I am,
> all that I have,
> and all that I do.
> Help me to surrender
> ever more fully to the Spirit.
> Lead me deeper into the Mystery
> of the Cross,
> the Cenacle
> and the fullness of Church.
> As you formed the heart of Jesus
> by the Spirit,
> form my heart
> to be the throne of Jesus
> in His glorious coming.

Our relationship with Mary is not a matter of option or mere private devotion. Our relationship with Mary is essential because of God's choice. This kind of attitude makes all the difference in the world in our attitude toward her and in our real devotion to her. The Second Vatican Council by the very fact of placing the Church's teaching on Mary in the key position of the eighth and final chapter of the Dogmatic Constitution on the Church ("Lumen Gentium"), shows us the key role of Mary in the Church and in our salvation. Mary's role is as Mother both of Jesus Christ and of His body the Church. We the Church are to be formed by Mary through the power of the Holy Spirit as Jesus our Head was formed. Mary as mother by the power of the Holy Spirit can only form Jesus and no other. So if we are born of her by the Spirit we are another "Jesus." We are the living icon of Jesus. We are His brothers and members of His body. To live as Christ we must be born as Christ.

When we accept the essential Maternal role of Mary in the Church and in the redemptive incarnation, then her other roles related to her Maternity, namely, mediatrix of all grace, and co-redemptrix fall into place. All of these, as well as the graces of her Immaculate Conception, Assumption and Queenship, are graces that are to be shared with the Church. What she has received is for all. "In the most holy Virgin, the Church has already reached that perfection whereby she exists without spot or wrinkle" ("Lumen Gentium," #65).

Father George Beaune, when he heard a teaching on Mary's graces, given at Bethany House, said with joy, "We shouldn't deny any grace to Mary, because all her graces are to be ours and if we deny her any graces we are denying them to ourselves!" God's great mysterious plan of redemptive incarnation is beyond all our imaginings. We are always in danger of limiting it with our attempts to rationalize it.

There is yet another role of Mary that we need to accept in a practical way and that is her Queenship and the victory over Satan that has been given to her. Her heel, her humility, her flesh that gave flesh to the Son of God by the Spirit will crush the head of Satan. The triumph of her Immaculate Heart, promised at Fatima, is the triumph over Satan and is the exultation of Jesus. There is so much that needs to be said about this victory. The point I want to make here, however, is that this again is an essential role of Mary and not a question of option. Especially in these times, that are so urgent, we need to accept, to understand, and to act in a meaningful and victorious way in this whole area of spiritual warfare, or else we as priests are just beating the air or playing tiddlywinks while Satan is destroying the Church and so many souls are being lost. This is a matter of the greatest urgency.

And the victory in this warfare goes not to those who are strong with human strength and determination, but to the little children in the arms of Mary. That is the paradox. If Mary is to form us, we need to live in the Heart of Mary. Here she forms us and prepares us for the battle with docility, humility, purity and the mercy of God. We as priests need a new and mature relationship with Mary. As adults we need to entrust our lives and formation to the woman to whom the victory is given, to the Woman who gave us the Victor, Jesus Christ.

Our part in this warfare is to entrust ourselves to her by consecration, to remain in her heart, to pray—especially the rosary—and to offer our sufferings. With these she will transform us into a powerful weapon for the salvation of the world. Ridiculous? Yes, but it is this humility and submission that will crush the pride and rebellion of Satan that we see in the present secularism and atheism of this generation. There is no other weapon given to us for the victory—no program. No great efforts and plans on our part can win the victory.

The victory is given to the Woman. This is God's plan and doing.

And what will be the sign of all this? "Then God's temple in heaven opened and in the temple could be seen the ark of the covenant. There were flashes of lightning and peals of thunder, an earthquake, and a violent hailstorm. A great sign appeared in the sky, a woman clothed with the sun, with the moon under her feet; and on her head a crown of twelve stars" (*Rev.* 11:19, 12:1). The sign given is "the woman." Then another sign, the dragon comes to do battle against the woman and her son. "Then war broke out in heaven; Michael and his angels battled against the dragon...he was hurled down to earth....They defeated him by the blood of the Lamb and by the word of their testimony... So rejoice you heavens...the earth came to the woman's rescue... Enraged at her escape, the dragon went off to make war on the rest of her offspring, on those who keep God's commandments and give witness to Jesus" (see *Rev.* 12:1-17). And so the battle continues on earth, but victory has been given to the woman. So, rejoice all you on earth—stand firm in your faith and enjoy the fight!

And what do you do if a brother priest finds all this foreign, outmoded and altogether too much? I would say, begin with a relationship with Mary.

What has been my advice to those who do not have a relationship with Mary? Hold on now—I tell them, "Go to Joseph!" Yes, to St. Joseph because as I mentioned earlier nobody I know had more trouble with Mary than Joseph! Mary got herself pregnant before they were married and Joseph knew that he didn't do it and he knew she was a holy girl. He was all upset about what to do with her. It took an angel of the Lord to let him know that what was in her was of the Holy Spirit. As the Acathist Hymn puts it:

> "Filled with a storm of contradictionary thoughts, the wise Joseph was greatly disturbed: until then, he had seen you a virgin, and now he suspected you of secret guilt, all blameless one! Learning that your conception was of the Holy Spirit, he cried out: *Alleluia!*"

Going to St. Joseph and asking his help will make us cry out, "Alleluia!"

Another approach I've taken in advising priests with difficulties with Mary is to tell them, "Ask Jesus about what He thinks of His Mother and have Jesus introduce you to His Mother!" Then the next step in this approach is to have them ask, "Jesus, show me Your love for Your Mother." I always have had positive and strong feedback on this approach. Then the further step is to ask, "Mary, show me your love for Jesus!" After that it's up to the Lord Jesus and to Mary to build the relationship.

If Jesus is Son of the Father and Son of Mary, who am I not to imitate Jesus and be like Him—a son of the Father and son of Mary.

In Jesus our Lord
and Mary our Mother,
Fr. George

13. TOTAL BAPTISM IN CHRIST JESUS

October 25, 1985
Holy Family Hermitage

Dear Father Ed,

The Lord be with you.
In the Liturgy the other day we heard the passage from Luke's gospel where Jesus describes His mission:

> "I have come to light a fire on the earth. How I wish the blaze were ignited. I have a baptism to receive. What anguish I feel till it is over. Do you think I have come to establish peace on earth? I assure you, the contrary is true; I have come for division" (*Lk.* 12:49-51).

The triplet that Jesus used to describe the purpose of His coming really struck me as something vitally important to us as priests.
Jesus said:

> I have come to **light a fire.**
> I have come to **receive a baptism.**
> I have come for **division.**

Jesus came to *light a fire!* "He will baptize you in the Holy Spirit and in fire" (*Lk.* 3:16 and *Matt.* 3:11). But first Jesus Himself was baptized in the Holy Spirit, while at the Jordan River. Then, "Jesus full of the Holy Spirit, returned from the Jordan and was conducted by the Spirit into the desert for forty days, where He was tempted by the devil" (*Lk.* 4:1). Jesus was baptized in the Holy Spirit to begin His mission of proclaiming the kingdom of God, beginning by encountering Satan. Jesus was totally immersed in the Holy Spirit to do the works of the Father. And Jesus came to baptize us in the same Holy Spirit—this was the very purpose of the coming of the Messiah. We too are to do the works of the Father but first we too must be baptized in His Holy Spirit.

Jesus came to *receive a baptism*. He was to be baptized in His own blood in the passion and death He predicted to His disciples. Jesus told James and John when they asked about sitting at His right and left in the kingdom, "You don't know what you are asking. Can you drink the cup I shall drink or be baptized in the same bath of pain as I?" "We can," they told him. Jesus said in response, "From the cup I drink you shall drink; the bath I am immersed in you shall share. . ." (*Mk.* 10:38). Jesus later told two of His disciples on the road to Emmaus: "Did not the Messiah have to undergo all this so as to enter into His glory" (*Lk.* 24:26), and then to His disciples in the upper room: "Thus it is written that the Messiah must suffer and rise from the dead on the third day" (*Lk.* 24:46).

Jesus had to be baptized in pain, baptized in His own blood to bring us mercy and salvation according to the Father's plan. Jesus calls us to that same baptism to the Father's will and plan, even to baptism in His bath of pain, to drinking His cup—what as priests we do at each Eucharist we offer. We too are to be baptized in the pain of the world and of our lives. We too are to be immersed in the blood of Jesus poured out for the remission of sins—poured out in the sufferings of the world today. Jesus has called us as priests; He has ordained us as priests in Him to continue His work of mercy and salvation. With St. Paul we too are ordained to say, "Even now I find my joy in the suffering I endure for you. In my own flesh I fill up what is lacking in the sufferings of Christ for the sake of His body, the church" (*Col.* 1:24). Christ's mission on earth is not yet completed because He has not yet suffered redemptively in you and me!

Jesus came for *division!* Jesus said I have not come to establish peace on the earth but division—right within the family—between children and parents. Jesus came to baptize us in His life as Son of the Father through a baptism in water that could establish new relationships with the Father and Himself our brother and Lord—such that all other relationships must be broken and set aside for the priority of Christ. Jesus put it in this way: "If anyone come to Me without turning his back on his father and mother, his wife and children, his brothers and sisters, indeed his very self, he cannot be My follower. Anyone who does not take up his cross and follow Me cannot be My disciple" (*Lk.* 14:26-27). Becoming a disciple of Jesus means a total break—division— but it also means a new life. By our water baptism we receive forgiveness of our sins, a new life as sons of the Father and we become members of His body—Jesus being Head, our Lord and our elder Brother and Mary, our Mother.

By being baptized into Christ we die to sin and self. Jesus Himself first showed us the way when He was baptized in water by John the Baptist, not because He had sinned and needed to be forgiven—but rather that He took on our sins to fulfill all of God's plan.

What impressed me about this insight was the totality of this three-fold baptism. First Jesus—totally filled with the Spirit, totally immersed in His own blood according to the Father's plan and totally given for the forgiveness of sin. Jesus was baptized in water, Spirit and blood in order that we too may be totally baptized in water, Spirit and blood— totally baptized into Him.

This is what our sacramental initiation into Christ should be! A total baptism in water for the forgiveness of sin, for sonship of the Father. Our Holy Orders then would be "an Ordination in the Holy Spirit," into the Spirit of Holiness to be an "alter Christus"—the presence of the "Baptized Christ"—Baptized in the Spirit, water and blood.

> "Thus there are three that testify, the Spirit and the water and the blood—and these three are of one accord" (*1 Jn.* 5:7-8).

As priests of Jesus Christ fully baptized into Him—fully baptized in the Spirit, water and blood—we would then like Jesus proclaim the purpose of our mission:

I have come to light a fire!
I have come to receive a baptism!
I have come for division!

It wouldn't take many priests like that to set the world on fire for the Lord!

In Christ Jesus Our Lord,
Fr. George

14. THE PRIORITY OF PRESENCE TO THE FATHER

October 25, 1985
Holy Family Hermitage

Dear Father Ed,

The Lord be with you!

You might get the impression that I have lots of time to myself in this hermitage. Well, as a matter of fact, the days and nights are so taken up with the things that "need" to be done that there could end up being no time—now that's a paradox! Fortunately, however, the main thing that "needs" to be done is to be *present* to the Lord. And there has been plenty of opportunity for that as long as I keep my priorities.

So it doesn't make much difference if you're in a parish or in a school, or in a hermitage; you have to set priorities for the use of your time. I set as my priorities three things, and this is the order of importance: 1) To listen to the Lord and be present to Him; 2) To intercede for the needs of the church and world; and 3) To do some writing on priesthood.

It is not easy, I find, to keep these priorities because my mind is so active at times from insights from prayer or from trying to write them down in these letters addressed to you. Also, my mind is very active in trying to respond to requests that come by mail. Some of these requests involve personal relationships and questions of ideals and goals which get me absorbed in prayer and discernment. Another area of energy output is prayer and sacramental ministry with penitents who come out to the hermitage. I find I'm getting more involved with their lives because I am interceding more for them that they may surrender their lives totally to the Lord.

At other times my mind is absorbed with an area in my personal life that needs healing—some fears or memories or areas of tensions in relationships, and anger; but again, "Thanks be to God in Christ Jesus our Lord" (*Rom.* 7:25) as the Liturgy today reminded me, all these areas of absorption are areas for healing, growth and intercession.

The special grace of this solitude is that whatever is absorbing me and my time I am learning to approach in a more peaceful and trusting way. Let me explain a way that is alive in me today. I've had several days of activity that involved my mind in writing, ministering with extended prayer that expended a lot of psychic energy. Today in my holy hour time I was aware of the Father and that the most pleasing thing for Him is that I am His son. I don't need to do anything or produce anything but be His son in the arms of Mary—like Jesus—that is the Father's great delight. I can rejoice that I am His son in the arms of Mary. I don't need to do or say anything else but be His son.

This is *the first priority* of this time of solitude—just to be the Father's son, present to Him, faithful to Him, listening to Him, alert and waiting upon Him, ready to do His will as He speaks.

The *second priority* of intercession flows from the first. Whatever is on my heart and mind I try to intercede for with an ejaculation of the heart, "Lord, have mercy on us and on the whole world." If the situation involves a relationship I may pray also "I repent of my wrong doing" and then cry, "Lord, have mercy." For more special needs I may pray the rosary or the Chaplet of The Divine Mercy and make a special intention in the Eucharist. I also have a number of people and communities who have asked for prayer. This brings me right back to the first priority: just *being* the son of the Father in the arms of Mary, like Jesus, pleases Him most. Our very lives in union with Him are an intercession.

And my *third priority* is writing on priesthood—that is, writing these letters to you in which I try to explain, first to myself, what is going on within me in these various insights and so develop them and also to remember them. I so easily forget—like the Israelites who had to be reminded over and over again, Remember Israel—"Take care not to forget the Lord, who brought you out of the land of Egypt, that place of slavery" (*Deut.* 6:12). Writing is for me a way of being present to what the Lord is saying to me. In writing, the insights are actually clarified, developed, as well as recorded. How well I remember your exhortation to me on a number of occasions, "Write down your ideas and experiences for the sake of others, even for those who years later can make use of them." Thank you, Father Ed. I'm trying to exercise this third priority as a response to your exhortation. I'm trying to record these insights while they are fresh so that I don't forget them and lose the initial spark of excitement.

And this writing has ben specifically on priesthood, either these letters to you or work on the *Diary of Sister Faustina* from which I am extracting the words of Our Lord and Sister Faustina directed to priests. The reason for this topic of priesthood is obvious—I've been involved with ministry to priests for these last fifteen years and there are a few things I want to and need to say. As you told me, "write down your experiences."

In sharing this letter with you I'm strengthened in my resolution to keep more clearly my first priority of presence to the Father as son in the arms of Mary like Jesus—in a word, "presence."

I now see more clearly how the other two priorities flow directly from this first of presence. I intend to intercede in the presence of the Father as His son and I intend to write more consciously in His presence.

> May you be filled with
> the presence of the Lord,
> Fr. George

15. THE PRIEST AS ICON OF JESUS

October 28, 1985
Holy Family Hermitage

Dear Father Ed,

The Lord be with you.
You know my love for ICONS.
I mentioned in one of my first letters that I have three special icons that are part of my prayer chapel. Mary, the Mother of God with the Christ Child embracing each other (The Theotokos of the Tenderness series); Lazarus being called forth from the tomb and being unbound, and the icon cross that spoke to St. Francis of Assisi. These three icons were also the focal icons of Bethany House of Intercession. I pray before them, stand before them and enter into the graces they present. I have also taught about these icons on a number of occasions.

But now, a new dimension is being added that has arisen from two sources: one from the current study of Leonid Ouspensky's *Theology of the Icon,* (St. Vladimir's Seminary Press, Crestwood, NY 10707, 1978), and the other from my prayer here at the hermitage. This new dimension has deeply touched my vision and prayer. Bear with me and I'll give you a summary of Ouspensky's book.

Here are some gems that touched me:

> "The icon is not just a simple image or a decoration, or even an illustration of the Holy Scripture. It is something greater. It is an object of worship and an integral part of the liturgy... The icon is one of the manifestations of the holy tradition of the Church, similar to the written and oral tradition" (p. 10).

Ouspensky gives a history of the apostolic and early developments through the period of Iconaclasts, then gives the orthodox teaching in response. Finally, he develops the meaning and content of the icon. Here are some more of his points:

> "Iconography is a way of expressing a tradition which existed from the beginning of Christianity, a way of conveying the divine revelation" (p. 163).
> "The Seventh Ecumenical Council asserts a divine inspiration for the icon, because the Holy Spirit inspires iconography. In both cases the source of inspiration is the same. This is why the icon is rightly called 'Theology in images,' parallel to theology in words. This is also why the Fathers of the Seventh Ecumenical Council say that Iconography was not at all invented by painters, on the contrary, it is an approved institution and a tradition of the Catholic Church" (pp. 163-164).

And now in regard to the appearance of the icon. The icon, like the Gospel, is, so to speak, in inverse perspective. The first shall be last; the meek and not the violent shall inherit the earth; and the supreme humiliation of the cross is truly the supreme victory. The strange and unusual character of the icon is the same as that of the Gospel. The form of icons sometimes borders on deformities which shock man, but the Gospel as well shocks man. Madness for the sake of the Christ and the sometimes provocative forms of icons express the same evangelical reality (see pp. 224-227). The inverse perspective is part of the "provocative" character. It is not an optical illusion, but it does draw us into the scene.

The inverse perspective of the icon is an important aspect. Because as we stand in prayer in the presence of the icon we are drawn into that grace. It doesn't "put us off." We are not in front of a portrait. We are in front of an icon that gives no obstacle to a direct contact with the sacred (see p. 217).

I am now at the point of my insight, which is based on sacred scripture; but in the light of the *Theology of the Icon,* it takes on deeper meaning. The insight is simply that:

I am to be a living ICON of Jesus.

I am to be transfigured and defined by the same Holy Spirit that transfigured Jesus on Tabor and I am to radiate His presence and grace. So as I become a living icon of Jesus, others looking at me should see Jesus and experience His grace and be drawn to Him. This is the work of the Spirit.

I have prayed specifically to be an icon of His mercy so that His mercy in me would draw people who see and hear me into His infinite mercy.

I am to be a saint!—in inverse perspective: "He must increase, while I must decrease" (*Jn.* 3:30). I am by baptism and ordination made into His image, now I must grow into His likeness.

In this light the Sacred Scripture on the IMAGE (the icon) becomes alive!

In *John* 12:20-23, we read that some Greeks came to Philip and put this request to him: "Sir, we should like to see Jesus." When brought to Jesus He tells of His glorification in being raised up and of the seed that must die to bear fruit. In *John* 14:9, again Philip is the go-between and asks Jesus, "Show us the Father!" Jesus responds, "Whoever has *seen Me* has seen the Father... Do you not believe that I am in the Father and the Father is in Me?" Then in *Colossians* 1:15, we have the declaration, "He is the image of the invisible God." Jesus is the ICON of the Father! When we look at Jesus, we see the Father.

Then in *2 Cor.* 3:18 through *2 Cor.* 4:10, we hear how we too are to be icons, icons of Jesus! "All of us gazing on the Lord's glory with unveiled faces are being transformed from glory to glory into His very image (ICON) by the Lord Who is the Spirit... Christ is the image of God... God Who has shone in our hearts, that we might make known the glory of God shining on the face of Christ."

We too are to be ICONS. As Jesus is the icon of the Father, we are to be icons of Jesus—this is the work of the Spirit through Mary:

> If we want to see the Father, look at Jesus.
> If we want to see Jesus, look at Mary.
> By looking at Jesus we begin to look like Jesus.
> By looking at Mary we begin to look like Mary and so, like Jesus.
> This is the work of the Spirit.

Lord, make us icons of Jesus.
Lord, make us icons of Mary.
Lord, make us icons of Mercy—
That we may reveal Your mercy to those who look
 at us.
This is the work of the Spirit.

Let Us make man in Our image, after Our likeness
 (*Gen.* 1:26).
This is the work of the Spirit,
The same Spirit by which
Jesus was conceived in the womb of Mary,
And the Spirit by which we are made icons of Jesus.

A footnote of special interest! I received a note from Father Seraphim Michalenko, M.I.C., this week telling me that he is on his way to Greece. He is to commission George Bogdanopoulos, one of the most renowned icon painters to undertake the painting of an icon of The Divine Mercy! What a beautiful response to a note I just recently sent to Father Seraphim asking him and encouraging him to try once again to have an icon made of The Divine Mercy—an icon with "inverse perspective" that would draw the one who venerates it into the grace of Divine Mercy. Father Seraphim asked for prayers for the whole process, first that he finds the man and that he undertakes the challenge and that he truly be inspired throughout.

As priests we especially are to be icons of Jesus our Eternal High Priest. We are to be united with Him, identified with Him, and radiate His priestly presence and power. Jesus prayed for us to the Father: "Sanctify them in the truth... And for their sake I consecrate Myself that they also may be consecrated in truth" (*Jn.* 17:17-19. RSV). As ordained priests we are the presence and power of Christ the High Priest—we are His icon. As people come to us they should see and experience Christ's merciful priesthood—His forgiving, His reconciling, His healing—His saving power.

In Jesus our High Priest,
Fr. George

16. THE PRIEST AS INTERCESSOR

October 31, 1985
Holy Family Hermitage

Dear Father Ed,

The Lord be with you!

The second priority of my sabbatical in solitude is intercessory prayer for the Church and world with a focus on priests and our renewal. In another letter I will reflect on the priest as victim-intercessor with Christ. Here, in this letter, I will consider praying for others. What I want to share is not the whole area of intercession but just the type of intercessory prayer that is alive in me now as I pray in the hermitage.

What is coming more and more to the surface is that my life, my whole life in union with the Lord, is intercessory. The more present I am to Him Who is Mercy Itself, the simpler and the more effective is my intercession. It is good to recall again what Blessed Paul Giustiniani said about intercession, "It is more important to know the one we are praying to rather than the one we are praying for." The point being that all flows from our union with God. He is the source of mercy and salvation.

These days I am peacefully aware of the situation in the Church and world and the needs of priests, religious and faithful. I say "peacefully aware" and that in itself is a grace! There is much less frenzy about the real urgency of the situation because I know that it is the Lord alone Who can bring about the resolution needed. He IS Lord and Master of all situations. I'm beginning to grow in trust of Him. So my part in the intercession is not to take charge of the situation but in simple trust to place the situation into the infinite ocean of His divine mercy. My part is to *ASK*.

ASK—Ask and you shall receive. Asking is the simplest, humblest, and most childlike thing I can do. Asking is my part in cooperating with the Lord in His Redemptive Incarnation. Asking is a beautiful way to exercise my human will in cooperation with the Divine Will, avoiding on the one hand Pelagianism (where I do it on my efforts) and on the other hand, avoiding Quietism (where I leave it all to God). Asking strikes a perfect balance. Ask—how much more will the heavenly Father give the Holy Spirit to those who ask him! So, too, we can grow in simplicity of asking for others.

During these weeks in solitude, I've simply been asking—asking for the Lord's mercy to come down upon the Church and world. I offer the Holy Eucharistic Sacrifice daily—asking for His mercy and His Holy Spirit on us and on the whole world. I pray the full rosary—a simple, humble prayer, asking Mary to pray for us sinners. I pray the Chaplet of The Divine Mercy, asking the Father to look upon the passion of His Son and have mercy on us and on the whole world.

I've been asking for the needs of individuals, and communities and families that I know and love and that have been recommended to my prayers. I have their names or letters on my intention board and I ask that they be filled with the mercy of God as I mention their names. I've been asking, too, for special intentions that come to mind and others that are of special interest: a brother priest in prison, a brother who needed to be freed of compulsive activity and receive the Holy Spirit.

So more and more simply I pray, "Lord, have mercy!" At other times it is an event or an intersection of events that I am involved in precisely in order that I may intercede. The Lord brought me to this intersection of events in order to intercede, and not to judge it, condemn it or to analyze it. If I don't intercede, then the Lord has to wait until another intercessor is ready and asks—and that further delays the plan of the Lord.

The Lord is looking for intercessors who are willing to ASK for His mercy when they see a need, or are involved in a need or are aware of a need. Would that the Lord would stir up His grace of intercession among us priests! So often we are asked for help and we give instead "good advice."

The people need the mercy of the Lord and we are channels of mercy by our ordination—we are intercessors by our Holy Orders. A minute of intercession is what is often needed rather than a half hour of counseling. Of course, at times both are needed.

The ministry of intercession is re-awakening in me—especially this past year. The Lord wants me to take on the burden of intercession and "twist His arm" for the needs of us priests.

During a conference held by John Wimber in Ann Arbor, Michigan, this September during a time of invocation of the Holy Spirit over the priests and pastoral leaders gathered around the foot of the stage, I received another supportive word. Father Pat Egan tapped me on the shoulder and gave me this prophetic word: "You will change people's prayer life, not by praying over them, but by explaining and showing them how to intercede." I tried this on several people during the conference itself and it seemed to work!

May these letters and the writing and teaching I've done before, stir up the grace of intercession among priests. It was a gift that came to me by way of Father Gerry Farrell, M.M. He and Father Joe Slaby, M.M. were led to intercede while on mission in Korea. This in turn was the source of our intercessory prayer idea at Bethany House of Intercession. For eight years we asked the Lord for renewal of priests, and in faith we believe He has and is answering those prayers.

Presently, I am experiencing a stirring up of this grace of intercession especially in the area of being present to the Lord, as mentioned in the beginning of this letter. Another grace is in the area of joining our suffering—ours and that of the world—with love, to that of Christ. But more on that in a separate letter because it's so vast and so important an aspect of our priestly intercession.

May the Lord bless you and fill you with His loving mercy and stir up within you the grace of intercession,

Fr. George

17. THE MYSTERY OF MERCY

November 4, 1985
Holy Family Hermitage

Dear Father Ed,

May the Mercy of the Lord flood you and may you receive it with joy. It's the third day of flooding rains. It's a sign of mercy. Paul goes on to explain God's plan of mercy:

> "Just as you were once disobedient to God and now have received mercy through their disobedience, so they have become disobedient—since God wished to show you mercy—that they too may receive mercy. God has imprisoned all in disobedience **that He might have mercy on all!**" (11:30-32).

God is so merciful that He wants to have mercy on all. He who is full of mercy, in fact is Mercy itself, wants to overflow with His mercy on all who receive it. God's great plan and desire is to have mercy on all—on all who receive it. This is the crunch—not all receive it. Some don't even know about it, some don't know how to receive it, others don't want to receive it. St. Paul then goes on to tell us how to respond to God's mercy and how to receive it and what to do with it. It is a whole practical catechesis on how to live as men of mercy. I think it is a lesson plan for us as priests to live out the mystery that we are—men of mercy.

First St. Paul bursts out into the magnificent canticle of divine mercy—it could be entitled "The Mystery of Mercy":

"How deep are the riches and the wisdom and the knowledge of God! How inscrutable his judgments, how unsearchable his ways! For who has known the mind of the Lord? Or who has been His counselor? Who has given Him anything so as to deserve return? For from Him and through Him and for Him all things are. To Him be glory forever. Amen" (11:33-36).

So the first step of response to God's mercy is to acknowledge God as God and as the source of all mercy and *praise* Him! Praise God from Whom all mercies flow.

Then Paul moves into the next response to mercy: "self-sacrifice."

"And now, brothers, I beg you through the mercy of God to offer your bodies as a living sacrifice holy and acceptable to God, your spiritual worship" (12:1).

This is a priestly response. It is a Eucharistic offering of our selves, even as Jesus offered His body given to Him on coming into this world so that He could do the Father's will (see *Hebrews* 10:5-11).

Following upon the first two responses to mercy—of praise and worship by sacrifice of self, Paul continues for the rest of the chapter to give a series of practical ways and attitudes in living a life of mercy. In a sense, he tells us how to be "merciful as our Heavenly Father is merciful" (see *Lk.* 6:36). He tells in a practical way how to be vessels of mercy (*Rom.* 9:23). Here is the list taken from *Romans* 12:2-21:

- Do not conform to this age,
- Be transformed by the renewal of your mind,
- Do not think highly of yourself,
- Estimate yourself by the measure of faith,
- Use the *gifts* given you—prophesy in faith, minister in service, teach with exhortation, give alms generously, rule with care, do works of mercy with joy.
- Love sincerely,
- Detest evil, cling to good,
- Love one another with affection and respect,

- Do not grow slack, but be fervent,
- Rejoice in hope,
- Be patient under trials,
- Persevere in prayer,
- Look on the needs of the saints as your own,
- Be generous in hospitality,
- Bless your persecutors, do not curse,
- Rejoice with those who rejoice,
- Weep with those who weep,
- Have the same attitude toward all,
- Put away ambitious thoughts,
- Associate with the lowly,
- Do not be wise in your own estimation,
- Never repay injury with injury,
- See that your conduct is honorable in the eyes of all,
- If possible, live peaceably with everyone,
- Do not avenge yourselves,
- If your enemy is hungry, feed him,
- Do not be conquered by evil, but conquer evil with good.

There are certain virtues in this list that stand out for me at this time of solitude because I've been praying for them and trying to practice them: praise, worship, purity, humility, works of mercy and joy. "Praise and worship," the first two major responses of St. Paul I've tried to be faithful to by being present to the Father as son in the arms of Mary, and in the offering of daily Eucharist and extending that offering in the presence of the Blessed Sacrament.

Purity—although the word is not used by St. Paul in this list, it is the next response listed and of course very common to Paul's teaching in his other letters (e.g., *Rom.* 1:18-32; *1 Cor.* 6:12-19). Here in *Romans* 12:2, Paul says not to conform to this age, not to offer our bodies to anyone but offer it as a living sacrifice (12:1). Then he goes on with other forms of purity—purity of mind, that we have God's mind (12:2) and purity of heart, that we seek God's will and please Him (12:2).

Humility is the next response of Paul (12:3). Without humility we cannot receive mercy. When we are filled with ourselves—self-concern, self-fulfillment—we are already filled and have no room for mercy. God can only be merciful to the humble.

Works of mercy—is a further response to mercy. We use the mercy we have received for the sake of others (12:4-11; 13:20-21).

Rejoice!—it is all God's gift (12:8, 12, 15).

Praise, worship, purity, humility, mercy and joy—these are the special graces the Lord has been awakening in me during these days. These are the very virtues of Mary herself! She by her purity and humility drew down the mercy of God. She responded to the presence of Mercy-Incarnate by praise, worship and rejoicing. Throughout these days I've been asking for the Lord's mercy in order that I may be a living icon of the merciful Jesus and an apostle of His mercy.

I've been increasingly aware that these are really Mary's gifts to us. She wants to share her immaculateness, her sinlessness that we too may be free of the great obstacle to God's mercy, namely, SIN—our sinful attachment to ourselves by our pride of not turning to Him in our need, and our impurity of heart, mind and body. Humility and purity are the two great weapons of Mary by which she crushes the head of Satan. It is no wonder that Mary is so concerned about humility and purity at her apparitions. As Mother she sees her children trapped by Satan, by pride, and by impurity—especially in this our age. Mary's triumph will be the triumph of God's mercy over these and all sin.

And so the great mystery of mercy—God's plan to have mercy on all—on all who call upon His name in humility and purity. God is so merciful that He cannot refuse mercy even to the greatest sinner who turns to Him for mercy.

The response of "rejoicing" is especially alive these days. I shared with Fr. Charles the other week that I don't remember such an extended time of joy in my heart. And recently, several things helped out considerably. The previous week Father John Bertolucci, my pastoral head, was here for sacramental ministry. I shared with him the tremendous graces and insights that I was receiving but that I also was asking for the gifts of purity and humility so that I don't take pride in these graces. He responded, "Don't be concerned about pride; rather, rejoice in the gifts God is giving you! So, for your penance," he said, "Rejoice over all the graces you have received!" This has been a real word of salvation for me—Rejoice! Rejoicing as the antidote to pride! So simple, so humble, so Marian! Thank you, Lord. Thank you, John.

The other week at Mass a gentle breeze of a grace went through my mind. "Make me holy!" I had just preached on the text in *Luke* eleven on asking, seeking, knocking... "how much more will the heavenly Father give the Holy Spirit to those who ask Him." I responded and expressed that desire as my own: "I ask you, Father, make me holy like Jesus, with the Holy Spirit." Later, during the thanksgiving time I heard within me, "Because you asked for holiness, I give you My greatest attribute, My mercy." My response was, "Thank you, Lord, now give me humility and purity like Mary's or else I will fall." Now I would add, "Give me joy!"

So in responding to God's mysterious mercy, His plan to have mercy on all, I am growing in the conviction of the need of praise, worship, purity, works of mercy and rejoicing—like Mary.

In the merciful Lord,
Fr. George

18. THE PRIEST AS VICTIM WITH CHRIST FOR OTHERS

November 5, 1985
Holy Family Hermitage

Dear Father Ed,

May the mercy of the Lord Jesus Christ fill you.

This letter is on one of the most challenging topics of our priesthood: *victims with Christ,* offering our sufferings and that of the world in union with Christ for the salvation of souls. It is an immense topic and it is a mystery of the first class. I'm approaching it in a peaceful state of mind and heart here in the hermitage. It has been a central part of my teaching, of my prayer and of my experience these last several years. I'm coming out of a three-year period of darkness and very much aware of sharing in the sufferings of Christ, and now have entered into a place of mercy. I'm looking at the same situation of suffering in the world as before, but with different colored glasses. The glasses are those of mercy. God's plan and desire is to have mercy on all—however, the chosen font of that mercy is the pierced heart of Jesus on the cross. I'm also aware of the five billion people on this globe of ours as well as all the souls in purgatory that are suffering. We all have suffering in our lives of some sort: tensions, fears, sickness, deprivations, sorrows and you name it! Suffering is a mystery beyond comprehension.

And yet we as priests are ordained to enter into this mystery. The fourth question of the ordaining Bishop to the candidate for priesthood asks: "Are you resolved to consecrate your life to God for the salvation of His people, and unite yourself more closely every day to Christ the High Priest, Who offered

Himself for us to the Father as a perfect sacrifice?" And the candidate answers: "I am, with the help of God." We are consecrated, that is, set aside as holy, set aside for sacrifice. And where is there sacrifice without pain and suffering?

A couple of years ago, I was writing an article on moving on to the full power of the priesthood, namely, on the cross in our lives, and I asked Father Benedict Groeschel, O.F.M. Cap., spiritual director of priests in the Archdiocese of New York, to read over the draft manuscript and comment on it. He responded by saying, "George, I tell it to you straight. Ninety percent of the priests won't know what you're talking about, but keep on writing and teaching!" (The second part of the article was published in *HOMILETIC and PASTORAL REVIEW,* June 1983, as "The Power of the Priesthood.") So I know that I'm writing on a very "unpopular" topic. Who wants to suffer and who wants pain?

But the point is that we *are* in fact suffering, here and now! It is not a question of some future possible suffering. It is the suffering of our heart, mind or body, our own suffering and that of the people. It is the kind of suffering which is my concern here, and should be the concern of all priests. What are we doing with the suffering and what are we doing for the suffering ones?

I've just made a survey of some of the most respected spiritual writers of our age and of my favorite saints and have come up with some surprising—if not startling—observations. I'll share some of these observations and insights on the topic of victimhood.

Before I give those observations I'll further point out that I am not speaking here of suffering with Christ for the sake of our own conversion or for our own purification or for our spiritual growth, or for our union with God—these are all essential and noble aspects of suffering and there are plenty of passages in Sacred Scripture and sacred authors to develop these aspects. Nor am I dealing here with the place of healing from sickness, whether physical or emotional. Healing is very much part of the Gospel. Healing reveals the great mercy of God; it frees us in order to do the works of mercy and to promote the kingdom. And healing also removes the obstacles to embracing the cross of Christ for others, and that with peace and joy. If we are not at peace and joy in our suffering, then we certainly need healing. Healing and suffering are both part of the Gospel. Here I am dealing with suffering for others.

The clearest and most authoritative source on this topic is the Apostolic Letter of Pope John Paul II, "The Christian Meaning of Human Suffering" (*Salvifici Dolores,* Feb. 11, 1984). There is so much in this letter that I'll just give the basic line of his presentation and recommend its study:

a) Christ sanctified suffering to be salvific by love (#14).
b) Christ invites us to share in His suffering with our love and so to sanctify and to save souls. Christ raised human suffering to the level of Redemption (#19).
c) At the Cross, Mary's role of consoling by her presence, of contributing by her compassion, and of "completing" in her flesh (see *Col.* 1:24) is the mission and vocation of the Church (#25).
d) "At one and the same time Christ has taught man to do good by his suffering and to do good to those who suffer. In this double aspect He has completely revealed the meaning of human suffering" (#30).

Here are two paragraphs that were especially helpful to me. John Paul II is commenting on St. Paul's Letter to the *Colossians* 1:24: "Now I rejoice in my sufferings for your sake, and in my flesh I complete what is lacking in Christ's afflictions for the sake of His body, that is, the church." Here Our Holy Father was speaking of the exceptional nature of the union of Christ with those who suffer.

> "For whoever suffers in union with Christ—just as the Apostle Paul bears his tribulations in union with Christ—not only receives from Christ that strength already referred to, but also completes, by his suffering, what is lacking in Christ's afflictions.

> "This evangelical outlook especially highlights the truth concerning the creative character of suffering. The sufferings of Christ created the good of

the world's redemption. This good in itself is inexhaustible and infinite. No man can add anything to it. But at the same time, in the mystery of the church as His body, Christ has in a sense opened His own redemptive suffering to all human sufferers. Insofar as man becomes a sharer in Christ's suffering—in any part of the world and at any time in history—to that extent he in his own way completes the suffering through which Christ accomplished the redemption of the world.

"Does this mean that the redemption achieved by Christ is not complete? No. It only means that the redemption, accomplished through satisfactory love, remains always open to all love expressed in human suffering. In this dimension—the dimension of love—the redemption which has already been completely accomplished is in a certain sense constantly being accomplished. Christ achieved the redemption completely and to the very limit; but at the same time *He did not bring it to a close.* In this redemptive suffering, through which the redemption of the world was accomplished, Christ opened Himself from the beginning to every human suffering and constantly does so.

"Yes, it seems to be part of the very essence of Christ's redemptive suffering that this suffering requires to be unceasingly completed..." (#24).

On the day he promulgated this apostolic letter, February 11, 1984, the Feast of Our Lady of Lourdes, Pope John Paul II held a Lourdes-type healing Mass in the Basilica of St. Peter's for over 800 sick from all over Italy. As they lay in stretchers and wheelchairs, accompanied by their assistants, he spoke of his apostolic letter to the sick and addressed them in these challenging words:

"Dear Sick! Offer your sufferings to the Lord with love and with generosity *for the conversion of the world!* Accept your pains with courage and confidence, also for all those who are suffering in the world because of religious persecutions, because of painful political and social situations, or who are victims of the corruption of customs and reigning climate of materialism and hedonism; or who wander without faith and without certainty in indifference or religious denial. You too, like Jesus on the Cross, can obtain graces of light, repentance, conversion and salvation for these brothers and sisters'' (#3).

I was encouraged and strengthened by this teaching of John Paul II. It confirmed the thoughts that I expressed in *Good News of Suffering: Mercy and Salvation for All,* (Liturgical Press, Collegeville, MN 56321, 1981), as I searched for the meaning and value of human suffering.

There is a clear message and challenge to us present in this teaching of Pope John Paul II. It is not easy to hear, nor is it easy to accept and apply. In fact, the surprise and even startling observations I spoke of earlier are that some of the great masters of the spiritual life of priests in our age do not deal with it in their major works—that is, either they do not develop it at all, or else they deal with it in a non-challenging, non-inspiring way, by quoting others.

Father Jordan Aumann, O.P., professor of spiritual theology at the Angelicum in Rome, in *Spiritual Theology,* (Our Sunday Visitor, Inc., Huntington, IN 46750, 1980), presents a splendid picture of suffering and redemptive suffering, giving both the scriptural and theological basis. Here is a sample paragraph:

> "One of the most tremendous marvels of the economy of divine grace is the intimate solidarity of all people through the Mystical Body of Christ. God accepts the suffering offered to Him by a soul in grace for the salvation of another soul or for sinners in general. It is impossible to measure the redemptive power of suffering offered to divine justice with a living faith and an ardent love through the wounds of Jesus. When everything else fails, there is still recourse to suffering to obtain the salvation of a sinful soul. The Curé of Ars said once

to a priest who lamented the coldness of his parishioners and the sterility of his zeal: 'Have you preached? Have you prayed? Have you fasted? Have you taken the discipline? Have you slept on boards? Until you have done these things, you have no right to complain' " (p. 171-172).

Wow! How do you like that response, Ed?

In dealing with offering oneself as a victim (by a vow) Father Aumann quotes Mother Marie Thérèse, foundress of the Congregation of Mary Reparatrix:

> "To be called a victim is easy and it pleases self-love, but truly to be victim demands a purity, a detachment from creatures, and a heroic abandonment to all kinds of suffering, to humiliation, to ineffable obscurity, that I would consider it either foolish or miraculous if one who is at the beginning of the spiritual life should attempt to do that which the divine Master did not do except by degree" (p. 175).

Father Aumann gives the theological basis for offering self as a victim of expiation: "The supernatural solidarity established by God among the members of the Mystical Body of Christ" (p. 175). He goes on to give a list of examples among the saints. Then he points out that this offering should never be permitted without a "persistent and irresistible motion of grace," and that the soul be well schooled in suffering and under the direction of a spiritual director. "Then, if God accepts the offering, the soul can become a faithful reproduction of the divine Martyr of Calvary" (p. 175)—an icon of Christ crucified.

This gives me an opportunity to make a very important distinction for us priests. When writing and teaching about "Priest as Victim," I am not dealing with this type of victimhood. I am not expecting or asking priests to take a vow, offering themselves as victims of expiation, and asking for sufferings—because this is a special vocation from God alone. What I am asking for and expecting is that priests offer for others, as expiation and atonement, the sufferings that they are in fact experiencing at this very moment—that they offer the burdens of each day. There are more than sufficient burdens of the day to offer—our own, and those of our people, and those of the whole world. This suffering is precious, is valuable; it is redemptive. Let us not waste it, but offer it in union with our Eucharistic sacrifice for the salvation of souls and the whole world.

Among the spiritual masters I consulted on this topic I turned to some of my favorites, who dealt with priestly spirituality.

- Father Eugene Boylan, O.C.R., *The Spiritual Life of the Priest,* (The Newman Press, Westminster, MD, 1953), has a chapter on "Victims with Christ" and one on "Self-Sacrifice" but neither of these deal with offering our sufferings for others.
- Dom Columba Marmion, O.S.B. in an anthology of his writings on *Suffering with Christ,* compiled by Dom Raymund Thibout, O.S.B., (The Newman Press, Westminster, MD, 1952), has two entries on suffering for others: he encourages a sister to yield herself to the wisdom and love of her Spouse, who is a Crucified God (p. 225); he encourages another, saying, "Christ is using her to lighten, vivify and save others" (p. 227).
- St. Joseph Cafasso in his collected conferences to priests, *The Priest the Man of God: His Dignity and His Duties,* (TAN Books and Publishers, Inc., P. O. Box 424, Rockford, IL 61105, 1971), does not treat the suffering of the priest as a conference topic in this collection.
- How beautifully the documents of the Second Vatican Council speak of offering our lives along with the offering of the Immaculate Victim, addressing priest and the laity ("Lumen Gentium," #34; "Sacrosanctum Concilium," #48; and "Prestyterorum ordinis," #5) and addressing the priests only: "So it is that while priests are uniting themselves with the act of Christ the Priest, they are *offering their whole selves* every day to God" ("Presbyterorum ordinis," #13). In the second chapter of "Lumen Gentium," on the "People of God," the council fathers conclude, ". . . the priest alone

can complete the building up of the Body in the Eucharistic Sacrifice... In this way the Church simultaneously prays and labors in order that the entire world may become the People of God" (#17).

The priest is a man of sacrifice. He is ordained to be in union with Christ who sacrificed Himself for us—for the salvation of the many. The fact that a priest is a man of sacrifice for others is verified by a long list of saints, mystics and holy men and women. I want to list some of those who have touched my life, and this with the hope that their words and example may stir the grace of our own priesthood:

Venerable Francis Liebermann, in his commentary on his Rule for missioners says, "True zeal, peaceable, humble and constant, sanctifies the soul, it does not become annoyed but tends to make us pray for souls who are in sin, offering ourselves to God for them and taking on ourselves the pain of their crimes" (*You have laid your hand on me: A message of Francis Liebermann for our time,* Alphonse Gilbert, C.S.Sp., Spiritan Research Centre, Rome, 1983, p. 107).

Conchita (the Servant of God, Maria Concepcion Cabrera de Armida) relates the words of the Lord to her "...one only Host, only only Victim, one only Priest immolating Himself and immolating me in your heart on behalf of the whole world. The Father pleased, will receive this offering presented through the Holy Spirit, and the graces of heaven will descend as rain on the earth. Here is the central nucleus, the center, the concrete ensemble of My Works of the Cross. It is evident that My immolation, in itself alone, suffices and more than suffices for appeasing God's justice. What is it, the purest Christianity, the flower of the Gospel? It is naught but uniting all victims in one single Victim, all suffering, all virtues, all merits in the One, that is, in Me, in order that all this be of worth and obtain graces! ... Has the Eucharist any other purpose than to unite bodies and souls with Me, transforming them and divinizing them?" (*Conchita: A Mother's Spiritual Diary,* Edited by M.M. Philipon, O.P., Alba House, NY 10314, 1978, p. 162).

This life and commentary of the works of Conchita have deeply influenced my thinking and attitude. Father Philipon places Conchita (1862-1937, born in Mexico and mother of nine children), because of the profoundness of her writings, in the category of St. Catherine of Siena and St. Teresa of Avila. This summer I finished reading this book a third time! I'm a great promoter of this book—I must have given away some two dozen copies.

Little Francisco and Jacinta of the Fatima apparitions (1917) offered all their little (and some not so little!) sacrifices for sinners, in response to Our Lady's instructions. I visited Fatima in October of 1984 and received a special grace. I wept at the tomb of Francisco—a patron of intercessors.

The Servant of God, Sister M. Faustina Kowalska (1905-1938) of Cracow, Poland, recorded her revelations on The Divine Mercy as well as her sacrificial offerings in her Diary (of VI notebooks). These revelations and the devotion to The Divine Mercy are part of my life. Daily I pray the Chaplet of The Divine Mercy as a priestly prayer of intercession. Here is just a little of what Our Lord said to her about her sufferings and what she did in response:

> "My child, you please Me most by your suffering. In your physical as well as your mental sufferings, My daughter, do not seek sympathy from creatures. I want the fragrance of your suffering to be pure and unadulterated..." (I, 124).
>
> "I desire that you make an offering of yourself for sinners and especially for those souls who have lost hope in God's mercy" (I, 133).

With the permission of her spiritual director, her response was an act of oblation that she repeated daily. It begins with an invocation of the Holy Trinity, the Blessed Mother and the angels:

> "I declare to the One Triune God that today, in union with Jesus Christ, Redeemer of souls, I make a voluntary offering of myself for the conversion of sinners, especially for those souls who have lost hope in God's mercy. This offering consists in accepting, with total subjection to God's will, all the sufferings, fears and terrors with which sinners are filled..." (I, 133).

She goes on to offer her consolations, her Masses and Holy Communions, penances and prayers, placing all her trust in the ocean of the Lord's mercy. Thanks be to God she prayed for priests as well.

St. Maximilian Maria Kolbe, O.F.M. Conv. (1894-1941) offered his life for the life of his fellow prisoner. On December 5, 1982, prior to the Mass in honor of the canonization of St. Maximilian celebrated in St. Patrick's Cathedral, NY, by Terence Cardinal Cooke, I had the opportunity to meet Franciszek Gajowniczek, the man Father Maximilian died for. I walked up to the front of the procession as it was forming behind the main altar and I greeted him in the Polish fashion with a double embrace and the greeting "Praised be Jesus Christ!" I received some of the grace of love that Maximilian passed on to Franciszek. By his very presence he is a witness of that sacrificial love which saved his life.

November 7, 1985

Alexandrina de Costa of Portugal (1904-1955) paralyzed from a thirteen foot fall when she escaped from her would be assaulters, offered her sufferings as a victim for conversion of sinners. For years, she regularly experienced the passion of Our Lord. For the last thirteen years of her life she lived on the Eucharist alone. She said the Lord told her, "you are living only by the Eucharist because I want the world to know the power of the Eucharist and the power of My life in souls."

Teresa Musco of Italy, who died just ten years ago, if I recall correctly, at the age of thirty-three. She offered her suffering of some 150 surgical operations and the passion of the Lord especially for priests!

Don Stefano Gobbi of Milan, Italy, has recorded his frequent locutions from Mary in the book *Our Lady Speaks to Her Beloved Priests,* (The Marian Movement of Priests, St. Francis, ME 04774). These locutions and the personal meetings with Don Stefano have influenced me deeply. The reading of this "diary" has become a daily teaching on how to live out my priesthood. One of the major practical teachings is on suffering, for example:

"Give me all the difficulties which you encounter, all the sufferings and the abandonment which you experience. Nothing comforts my Immaculate and Sorrowful Heart more than a suffering which is offered to me out of love by my Priest-sons.

"Even Jesus willed to offer to the Father all His sufferings through and with me. And it was thus that, offering my Son freely to the Father, I became true Co-Redemptrix.

"Let these children of mine offer me all their sufferings, all their misunderstandings, all their difficulties. This is the greatest gift that they can make to me, because thus they allow me to carry out in time—in this, your time!—my task as Mother and Co-Redemptrix. I will save many souls redeemed by Jesus, but at present so far away from Him, because my sons, together with me, will pray for them.

"Oh, all I want of them is prayer and suffering: this is how they will comfort my Heart and respond to His great plan of Mercy which I am about to realize through them" (April 1, 1974)

This has been a very long letter, Ed, but it also is probably the most important letter of all those I have written. God is revealing to us His plan which is a mystery—a mystery of mercy, and Mary, and we are part of it. Our suffering offered with love is part of this plan. It is a mytery—it is a mystery of mercy on the whole world. It has to do with the preparation for the Lord's coming again. The Church today, and we with it, is in the midst of this mystery, this travail, this crucifixion for the salvation of the world. It is a great moment of mystery and mercy and I don't want to miss out on it and I don't want my brother priests to miss out on it. Now is the time for mercy, now is the time for entering into this great mystery with Mary, in her arms, in her heart as children and yet as mighty warriors. I wish I had more words to express this sense of God's mighty and mysterious and marvelous plan of mercy. He is preparing the Church and us for something so marvelous that: "Eye has not seen, ear has not heard, nor has it so much as dawned on many what God has prepared for those who love Him. Yet God has revealed this wisdom to us through His Spirit" (*I Cor.* 2:9-10). Some day when we grasp this mystery of God's wisdom we will sing out with St. Paul:

> "How deep are the riches and the wisdom and the knowledge of God! How inscrutable His judgments, how unsearchable His ways! For "who has known the mind of the Lord? Or who has been His counselor? Who has given Him anything so as to deserve return?" For from Him and through Him and for Him all things are. To Him be glory forever. Amen" (*Rom.* 11:33-36).

Amen?
Amen! and Alleluia!

By way of conclusion, I am enclosing a letter of Pope John Paul II to Father Philip Bebie, C.P., a personal friend of mine who is dying of a rare liver cancer. I spent a couple of hours sharing and praying with him just before coming to the hermitage in August. Our visit centered on the mystery of mercy and Mary.

May the King of Mercy bless you and the Mother of Mercy embrace you,

Fr. George

Enclosed: Letter of John Paul II to
Father Bebie, C.P.

P.S. Father Philip Bebie died October 30, 1986. The Sunday before his death I led the chaplet of Divine Mercy in his hospital room. He responded in a subdued but distinct voice. We blessed each other and said good-bye until we saw each other in Heaven.

To Father Philip Bebie, C.P.

I have received your letter informing me of the state of your health and of your intention to offer your life in Christ for His Church, for me and for all priests. In the name of our Lord Jesus Christ I thank you for your willingness to accept with resignation and love the dispositions of God's Providence. Be assured that your sacrifice, united to Christ's saving Passion, will contribute greatly to the application of the merits of Redemption to the hearts of God's people.

At this time I commend your intentions and your future to the Immaculate Heart of Mary, praying that she will strengthen you to the end with her motherly love. With affection in Christ Jesus I send you my special Apostolic Blessing.

From the Vatican, August 22, 1983

(Signed) Joannes Paulus II

19. THE IDENTITY OF THE PRIEST

November 8, 1985
Holy Family Hermitage

Dear Father Ed,

Over the years I've reflected on and taught on the identity of the priest. I know the basic identity comes from Jesus Christ the Eternal High Priest. There is only one priest, Jesus Christ, the Holy One of God. But today I gained a deeper insight into our priesthood based on a deeper insight into Jesus as the Messiah. The source of this grace came from the pages of a book called *The Communion of Love*, a collection of articles by Matthew the Poor (St. Vladimir's Seminary Press, Crestwood, NY 10707, 1984). Father Matta El-Meskeen (Matthew the Poor Man) belongs to the Coptic (Egyptian) Orthodox Church. He is the spiritual father in the Monastery of St. Macarius in the desert of Scetis (Scete), Wadi El-Natroon and a mystic of profound spirituality.

In a clear and inspiring way Matthew the Poor shed new light for me on the basic teaching concerning Jesus as priest, prophet, and king, a teaching which I've regularly used as the foundation in explaining our priestly identity. Here is a summary of what he says:

God revealed Himself in the Old Testament in a historical method using three components:

1) establishing the people as a nation under judges, rulers and **kings** so that through them the people would perceive God's perfect direction of affairs,
2) giving laws and regulations and anointed **priests** to teach and draw them to God, so that they could sense Him through purification,

3) giving prophecies and spiritual direction concerning the future through **prophets** so that by repenting and drawing near to God they might know Him.

The amazing thing is that each of these three components appears in every book of the Bible, and deep study and meditation show that they constitute a clear and perfect plan with a logical method and a clear purpose (p. 44). The divine plan that lay behind the establishment of this living body (a people led by a divinely anointed king, served by a divinely appointed priest, and inspired by a prophet who spoke by the Holy Spirit) may be summarized as God's desire to reveal Himself to the world through this living body that progressed through time and over many generations (p. 45).

And so the Messiah was reckoned from the beginning to be: 1) the everlasting King who was the culmination of all kings, 2) the Priest who brings eternal reconciliation with God and 3) the Prophet to whose (who was) coming in the fullness of time (see p. 45-46).

In the period before the birth of Christ the rabbis collected 458 Messianic references in the Bible. They insisted that there was no prophecy outside the Christ:

> "All the prophets prophesied only concerning the days of the Messiah. It was only immediately before the coming of Christ that the rabbis got absorbed in intricate expositions and wandered off in fanciful deductions" (p. 49).

Jesus came as the fulfillment of the Messiah's role as King, Priest, and Prophet. He also came as the fulfillment of the characteristics of Israel as first-born son and servant (p. 46).

This teaching of Matthew the Poor helped me to understand that now the church, both people and priests, are the sharers in who Christ is—each in their own way. When read in this light, the words of St. Peter come alive in a new way:

> You, however, are a "chosen race, a royal priesthood, a holy nation, a people He claims for His own to proclaim the glorious works" of the One who called you, from darkness into His marvelous

light. Once you were no people, but now you are God's people; once there was no mercy for you, but now you have found mercy (*1 Ptr.* 2:9-10).

We are kings, priests and prophets in Christ, proclaiming His mercy. Jesus, the King of mercy, the Priest of mercy, the Prophet of mercy now shares His mercy with us that we might be as merciful as our heavenly Father is merciful and proclaim His glorious works. As a kingly—priestly—prophetic people we share in the promises and revelations of the Old and New Testament. Our priestly roots are in old covenant priesthood and our vine is the new covenant.

I now appreciate even more what Pope John Paul II, while still Archbishop of Cracow, said in regard to the Second Vatican Council in his commentary, "Sources of Renewal: Implementation of Vatican II," (Karol Wojtyla, Harper Row, 1979), when he made this sweeping statement about the Council and priesthood:

> "It can be in a sense said the doctrine concerning Christ's priesthood and man's share in it is at the very centre of the teaching of Vatican II and contains in a certain manner all that the Council wished to say about the Church, mankind and the world" (p. 225).

We are priests not only by Baptism but more specifically by the sacrament of Holy Orders: "they are marked with a special character and are so configured to Christ the Priest that they can act in the person of Christ the Head," ("Presbyterorum Ordinis," #2). The phrase "in the person of Christ the Head," in the context of the Holy Sacrifice, really helped me to grasp our role as ordained priests. Pope John Paul II in writing to all bishops and priests on the Eucharist made an important clarification for me on this point:

> "The priest offers the Holy Sacifice *in persona Christi;* this means more than 'in the name of' or 'in the place of' Christ. *In persona* means in specific sacramental identification with 'the eternal High Priest' (opening prayer of the second votive Mass of the Holy Eucharist) who is the Author and princi-

pal Subject of this Sacrifice of His, a Sacrifice in which, in truth, nobody can take His place. Only He—only Christ—was able and is always able to have 'propitiatory power' before God, the Trinity, and the transcendent Holiness. Awareness of this reality throws a certain light on the character and significance of the priest celebrant who, by confecting the Holy Sacrifice and acting 'in persona Christi,' is sacramentally (and ineffably) brought into that most profound sacredness, and made part of it, spiritually linking with it in turn all those participating in the Eucharistic assembly" (*Dominicae Cenae,* #8, February 24, 1980).

In light of the insights of Matthew the Poor and of John Paul II, the description of the priest given by the Second Vatican and incorporated into the ordination rite takes on still deeper significance:

> By sacred ordination and by the mission received from their bishops, priests are promoted to the service of Christ the Teacher (read Prophet), the Priest and the King (read Pastors), (developed in chapter two of the document). They share in His ministry of unceasingly building up the Church on earth into the People of God, the Body of Christ, and the Temple of the Holy Spirit (I like that three-fold description of the Church, making it Trinitarian!) ("Presbyterorum Ordinis," #2).

Our identity as priests is found in this definition by the Church. We are prophets, priests, and pastors in Christ Jesus who is *the* Prophet, *the* Priest, *the* Pastor.

Our identity as priests is very clearly stated by the Church. But the priority of the three-fold role of Christ in our lives is a problem for some priests. Again, the documents of the Second Vatican Council make it clear, if they are properly understood and set in juxtaposition.

So what I understand is being said in "Presbyterorum Ordinis" about the priorities of a priest participating in the three-fold role of Christ is this. We start with the prophetic role, preaching and teaching the Gospel of Jesus Christ. This prophetic role prepares for and leads to the chief role of the priest, namely, the priest acting as priest in the Eucharistic Sacrifice. From this priestly role flows the pastoral love, the shepherding of God's people. The chief priestly role of sacrifice begins with the prophetic word and overflows with merciful ministry. The priestly dimension is our chief priority.

In a way, our identity is one of the mercy in Christ Jesus, Jesus who is king of mercy, offers Himself as Incarnate Mercy in a sacrifice of mercy for the merciful salvation of His sheep. As ordained priests we share in this ministry of mercy. By the same Holy Spirit we are configured to Christ and are to be living icons of the merciful King and Shepherd, of the merciful Priest Who laid down His life for His sheep, and of the merciful Prophet Who calls each by name, cares for them, and leads them. By the mercy of the Father and of the Lord Jesus Christ we are what we are, priests in Christ Jesus, our Prophet, Priest, and Pastor. By the mercy of God we are to be as merciful as our Heavenly Father is merciful.

Who are we as priests? We are men of mercy and ministers of mercy so that God may have mercy on all.

A final and related point in regard to our identity as priests. Some priests are concerned about their relationship to the laity. How close? How separated? Again the Vatican document speaks clearly to me on the question:

> By their vocation and ordination, priests of the New Testament are indeed set apart in a certain sense within the midst of God's people. But this is so, not that they may be separated from their people or from any man, but that they may be totally dedicated to the work for which the Lord has raised them up. They cannot be ministers of Christ unless they are witnesses and dispensers of a life other than this earthly one. But they cannot be of service to men if they remain strangers to the life and conditions of men ("Presbyterorum Ordinis," #3).

The purpose of being "set apart" is not to separate but to totally dedicate, totally consecrate. We are ordained to a heavenly ministry—to do on earth what is already done in Heaven. This heavenly ministry is a great topic that has me excited and I'll tell you about that in another letter.

Ed, may the Lord in His mercy make you more and more a man of mercy and a minister of mercy.

In His Mercy,
Fr. George

20. LAMENTATION

November 9, 1985
Holy Family Hermitage

Dear Father Ed,

Lamentation? Yes, we priests need to discover or re-discover how to lament for ourselves and for our people. The text of Joel used in our Ash Wednesday Liturgy comes to mind:

> Between the porch and the altar let the priests, the ministers of the Lord, weep and say, "Spare, O Lord, Your people and make not Your heritage a reproach with the nations ruling over them" (*Joel* 2:17).

and Joel again:

> "Gird yourselves and weep, O priests, wail, O ministers of the altar! Come, spend the night in sackcloth O ministers of my God!" (*Joel* 1:13).

Yes, the situation in the Church and world is such that it calls for lamentation—calling down God's mercy on our misery.

Here is a description of a recent experience of my lamentation for priests called: "Lamenting: The Descent to Hell." I wrote it down immediately after it happened so that I wouldn't forget it and also to deepen my awareness of the need of lamentation. It has special relevance to me in the hermitage, since my second priority in being here is to intercede. Following the description of this experience, I will share with you the words of Father William Johnston, S.J., formerly of Sophia University in Tokyo, now in Manila, P.I., and his picture of lamentation for the evil and darkness in the world.

I have a great respect for Father Johnston. I had two occasions to share and pray with him, one here in the U.S.A. and the other in Japan. While in Japan he lamented to me concerning the number of Christians who came out to Japan to search out eastern mysticism and yet they did know Jesus Christ and their own Christian Mysticism!

LAMENTING: The Descent to Hell

Jesus died and descended to Hell!

Jesus was buried among the dead. He descended to Sheol, the place of the dead to raise those awaiting His resurrection; to preach to those in prison (see *1 Peter* 3:19, and 4:6).

Very early this morning, before dawn, I awoke and began to weep and sob for the condition of so many priests. It was a deep sobbing and cry to God, "What the hell is goin on!?" As time passed I was drawn to get out of bed and go downstairs, before the Lord. And I lamented freely, I cried out in pain and anger!

Finally, the breakthrough for me. I could get angry at God! I complained to Him and I scolded Him as my most dear Lord, as my Bridegroom! Then, as it were, turning to the Father, I said: "Father! Your Son descended to Hell! Isn't that enough! Look at Him and have mercy on us priests! You cursed your Son, must we be cursed too?! (see *Gal.* 3:13).

What freedom came in lamenting to God! I was so supported by yesterday's teaching of Father Raniero Cantalemessa, O.F.M. Cap., one of the speakers at the Priests and Deacons Conference here at the University of Steubenville. He encouraged us to pray with boldness, to intercede for our people, like Abraham, like Moses, like Job. When our heart is right with the Lord, then our lips can speak freely to God. But if it is the other way around—our lips are with God but our hearts far away—then it is hypocrisy.

As I continued to lament I looked at the sacred scripture, especially the Gospel according to St. Matthew where he describes the death of Jesus. The earth quaked, the veil of the temple was torn, tombs were opened and saints of old were raised from their tombs and visited many in Jerusalem (cf. *Matt.* 27:51-54).

Jesus died, was buried and descended to the dead (Apostles Creed). I began to be very aware of the death and burial of Jesus. Jesus emptied Himself to the utmost. The Byzantine icon of Good Friday and Holy Saturday came to mind, so I brought it out of the cabinet and placed it on the mantelpiece in my room. The icon portrays the upper torso of the crucified Jesus standing in the tomb with the inscription: "Extreme Humility!"

This is Extreme Humility! This is the descent to the "Still Point" of the turn around. This is the absolute bottom of the pit! From here, the only possible direction is up, and that is resurrection.

But this "still point" of the extreme bottom, this descent to Hell is where so many priests are called to be! This is the moment of identification with Christ Jesus, our Eternal High Priest, Who descended to Hell for our salvation. Here is the place we cry out, "Father, look at the broken body of Your Son! Have mercy on us and on the whole world." Here as priests we are to weep and mourn for the Body of Christ is broken! Here is our present place of lament and intercession for the whole Church.

Oh, if we could only learn to lament! The Spirit teaches us in both the Old and New Testament to lament as well as to praise God—we see this in the psalms, in the prayer of Abraham, Moses, and the prophets like Jeremiah, and Job.

To lament is a fascinating type of prayer because in fact we do indeed lament often and freely, but to the wrong persons. We gripe like hell to one another—and we call it "bitching." But if we direct our griping to God, then it is lamentation. This, of course, presumes a very fundamental reality, namely, that we are in a covenant relationship with God. We radically trust in Him, so that then we are free to complain and argue with Him.

For me, this experience of this morning's lamentation was a "coupe de main"—a stroke of genius, a moment of breakthrough. The other evening I gave a teaching on the "Priest as Intercessor" to those gathered at the Steubenville Conference. It was really my life's testimony, a testimony of my crushed heart in interceding for priests, my life's teaching on victim intercession. My sense afterwards was a numbness, not remembering what I really said, but feeling as though my guts were poured out—I had no more to share; I shared my brokenness. So many priests throughout the following day came up to hug me for touching their crushed hearts. And now for me, this moment of lament, helped me in the most difficult aspect of intercession as victim—which is the pain of not knowing whether this pain is really intercessory and salvific or not. Am I just kidding myself? Is it just a game?... No, it is the descent to Hell!

Hell is where the broken priests are and it is where the broken people are and it is from there we lament. And it is by the power of Christ's descent to death, to the tomb and to Hell that we can lament—"Father look at the Body of your Son, broken and in Hell and have mercy on us and on the whole world."

Thanks be to God that in the pit of Hell we can cry out with the psalmist:

> "Out of the depths I cry to you, O Lord.
> Lord, hear my voice!" (*Ps.* 130)

Thanks be to God, that the Spirit who raised Jesus from the pit of death will raise us up! (see *Rom.* 8:11).

The Byzantine Church celebrates this victory with the Resurrection icon, which portrays Jesus gloriously risen from the tomb, seizing Adam in one hand and Eve in the other and drawing them up out of the shackles of the tomb. The Byzantine Church celebrates the descent of Jesus to the pit of death as the moment of the greatest power of the paschal mystery. Jesus, in His descent to and ascent from the dead, conquers the territory of Satan, of sin and death itself, the final enemy. Over and over again the victorious chant of Easter is sung:

> Christ is Risen from the dead!
> He has crushed death by His death
> and bestowed life upon those who
> lay in the tomb. (Easter, Byzantine Liturgy)

By His descent and ascent Jesus conquers all creation, all space and time.

St. Ephrem, known as the "harp of the Spirit" sings of the victory of His descent and ascent:

> He sprinkled dew and life-giving rain
> on Mary, the thirsty earth.
> Like a seed of wheat He fell again to Sheol,
> to spring up as a whole sheaf, as the new Bread,
> Blessed is His Offering!

From on high He came down as Lord,
from the womb He came forth as a servant.
Death knelt before Him in Sheol,
and Life worshiped Him in His resurrection.
Blessed be His victory!
   (St. Ephrem, *Hymns on the Resurrection,* no. 1).

During my first stay in the hermitage I read a very significant book, highly recommended by Father Bohdan who sent it to me. It is called *Christian Mysticism Today,* by William Johnston, S.J., (Harper and Row, 1984). This book brought home to me in a striking way the need of lamentation. In it, Father Johnston deals with the Christian roots of mysticism and he says unhesitatingly that there are three such: 1) The Word of God in Sacred Scripture, 2) The Sacraments, particularly the Eucharist, and 3) the Word of God in the community called Church (p. 9). In dealing with the presence and absense of God he confronts the question of the mystic going through Hell and its meaning vis-a-vis the situation in the world. By way of explanation Father Johnston says that "Christian mysticism" is nothing other than an entrance into the baffling mystery of love and the experience of its transforming power" (p. 17). Here is his section on lamentation:

> I hear you say: "Presence and absence! Wonderful! But are not these mystics engaged in a pious and loving ego-trip, far from the immense problems of our troubled country? What about nuclear war? What about pollution of the atmosphere? What about starvation and oppression and torture?"
> Let me explain. Every step of the way, the mystics are close not only to God but to the whole human family. Even (indeed especially) in those dark nights of seeming despair when God seems absent and Hell lies open—even then they are very, very close to us.
> For the fact is that our modern world is in a dark night. And the evils of hunger and war and oppression are symptoms of an even deeper evil: rejection of God and deliberate choice of darkness. Many, many people are without faith, without hope, with-

out love, lost in a morass of despair, wandering in the night, lost in this world—and who knows if they will be lost in another?

And in their dark nights the mystics go through Hell, not for themselves but for the world. They taste the very despair their contemporaries taste; the resonate with the agony of those who believe that God is really dead. They are like Jesus in Gethsemani; they cry out: "Lama sabacthani!" ["why have you forsaken me"] and their unwavering faith is a light to a faithless world.

To us their lives may look irrelevant—they themselves feel totally irrelevant—that is part of their darkness. But they are at the center of the titanic struggle for the salvation of the world. They are a beacon to all of us. Through them we are saved" (p. 52).

I resonate with Father William Johnston's description and I think it is a challenge for us priests to lament for the sin of the world, crying out for God's infinite mercy: "Father, for the sake of the passion of Your Son, for the sake of His passion continued in the countless men and women of today, have mercy on us and the whole world." We priests have the power of Jesus Christ Himself to call down the mercy of God. We need to lament!

In the Lord's mercy,
Fr. George

21. A MYSTERIOUS, HEAVENLY PRIESTHOOD: THE IDENTITY OF THE PRIEST: PART II

November 11, 1985
Holy Family Hermitage

Dear Father Ed,

Last October while in Rome for the World-wide Retreat for Priests and Deacons I heard Father Raniero Cantalamessa, O.F.M. Cap., the preacher to the papal household, describe the priest as mysterious: "The priest is both minister and mystery." This phrase of his stayed with me and has grown into another way of describing our priesthood, one that gives us a heavenly identity.

Let me explain it this way. Before Vatican II, generally, we as priests were described in terms of a hierarchy: pope, bishops, priests, deacons, and people. This is true but it is not the only way to describe the priesthood. Since Vatican II the generally used term to describe us has been a "ministerial priesthood." This is also true but it is also not the only way to describe the priesthood.

There is a third way to describe who we are. We are a mysterious, mystic, heavenly priesthood. And this is also true but it's going to need some explanation!

Our identity comes from Jesus Christ our eternal High Priest. As High Priest, Jesus, Son of the Father and Son of Mary, emptied Himself through His passion and death on the cross, offered Himself by the eternal Spirit as the Unblemished Lamb (*Heb.* 9:14) to the Father to cleanse us of our sins. Raised by the Father by the same Holy Spirit, Jesus entered the Holy of Holies, not the Holy of Holies made by the hand of Moses which was a copy of what he saw in Heaven, but He entered the real and eternal Holy of Holies, Heaven itself, and came before the mercy seat of His Father as He sprinkled His very own blood for the forgiveness of our sins. Jesus, our eternal High Priest, entered Heaven for us; He opened the way and approached the throne of God with His own precious blood. Jesus our High Priest is before the very throne of God the Father. And now we await His coming again, His coming out of the Holy of Holies with the victory of salvation, with mercy for all who eagerly await Him (*Heb.* 9:28). We as priests find our identity with this mysterious, mystic, heavenly, and eternal High Priest, Jesus Christ our Lord.

We are a heavenly priesthood! Like Jesus and with Jesus we are to be in Heaven before the throne of God, for the sake of His people. Like Jesus and with Jesus we are to offer the sacrifice of mercy, His body and blood for the forgiveness of sin. Like Jesus and with Jesus we are to plead for mercy on us and on the whole world.

This dimension of the priesthood came alive for me in the Liturgy this Sunday in the text of *Hebrews* 9:24-28: "Jesus entered Heaven itself that He might appear before God on our behalf" (vs 24). I also realized that this is only one dimension of our priesthood but it is a very significant one in our day because it has been so neglected. When is the last time that you read of this dimension?

As I reflected on this heavenly dimension of priesthood I did so in conjunction with the two other descriptions: the ministerial and the hierarchical priesthood. I looked for a scriptural basis for our identity with Christ in all three of these dimensions and eureka! I found them in terms of commands. We are told to be merciful as our heavenly Father is merciful (*Lk.* 6:36). This is what the ministerial priesthood is about: being merciful to those in need of mercy, being channels of God's mercy to all of us sinners, to all in misery. "Be merciful" describes the identity and role of the ministerial priesthood. Then in regard to the hierarchical dimension of our priesthood I realized that this dimension is one of the humble service as brothers. The pope is "servant to the servants of God." The real meaning of hierarch is "one who leads the worship, a servant of the people and a brother to his brother servants." And another command based on the attitude and character of Jesus is: "Be humble." Be humble as Jesus is humble and learn from Him (*Matt.* 11:29) because His attitude is one of humility (*Phil.* 2:5-11) as He emptied Himself even to death on a cross.

This then sets the stage for the third dimension. How are we to be like Jesus our Heavenly High Priest? Again a command: "Be holy because I am holy" (*1 Ptr.* 1:16 and *Lk.* 19:2). We imitate Christ and identify with Him as a heavenly priesthood by being holy as He is holy and that by the same Holy Spirit. We find our identity in the Holiness of Christ Himself!

So our identity is in Jesus Christ who is Holy, Merciful and Humble. This means that as priest I am to be holy, merciful and humble—there is no escaping this fundamental identity and reality. This picture of our priesthood gives us a whole program of spirituality and ministry.

The people need holy, merciful and humble priests. They want, look for, and need priests who know God, love God and are ministers of His mercy. The people want to know God through us. We are to introduce them to the Lord and bring them ever closer to Him. If we don't know Him...then what?! We are above all a heavenly priesthood—with Jesus our heavenly High Priest. From there the faithful eagerly await His coming in mercy—they expect the same from us.

(Continued) November 12, 1985

Eureka! I found confirmation of this mysterious, mystical, heavenly priesthood in the Ordination Rite of the Priest, as well as confirmation of the hierarchical and ministerial dimensions of the priesthood. The very text of consecration, in fact the essential words invoke the Spirit of holiness upon the candidate in the context of his hierarchical relationship to the bishop as co-worker and of his ministerial relationship to the people:

> "Almighty Father,
> grant to this servant of Yours
> the dignity of priesthood.
> ***Renew within him the Spirit of holiness.***
> As a co-worker with the order of bishops
> may he be faithful to the ministry
> that he receives from You, Lord God,
> and be to others a *model* of right conduct"
> (Rite of Ordination of a Priest).

This is the special prayer of the Sacrament of Holy Orders. The Holy Spirit grants to this servant the dignity of a holy priesthood. How rightly this sacrament is called Holy Orders. The prayer of the ordaining bishop is that this priest be a model of right conduct, a model of what is in Heaven, a living icon of Jesus Christ eternal High Priest.

Further confirmation of the mysterious and mystical priesthood comes from the exhortation of the bishop to the newly ordained priest in handing him the gifts of bread and wine:

> "... Know what you are doing, and imitate the mystery you celebrate: model your life on the mystery of the Lord's Cross."

This confirmation of the heavenly dimension of our priesthood makes this an especially important aspect of our priesthood. We must be holy, we have no choice—we must be living icons of Jesus our High Priest in Heaven. By His Holy Spirit we are to be like Him—holy, humble and merciful.

And how holy, humble and merciful is the Lord? Let me put it this way: The all Holy One, Jesus, is so transcendent, beyond, and ineffable that all we can do is cry with the angels "Holy, Holy, Holy." Yet this all Holy One of God emptied Himself even to death, death on a Cross (*Phil.* 2:8) and was buried and descended to the dead in extreme humility. But God the Father showed Him mercy and raised Him all the way to the Holy of Holies and "made both Lord and Messiah this Jesus..." (*Acts* 2:36). The measure of God's mercy is the "distance" between His Transcendent Holiness to His extreme humility—that is infinite mercy!

May the Lord Jesus, our eternal Heavenly and High Priest fill you with His holiness, His humility and His infinite mercy through the Holy Spirit.

Fr. George

22. MOVING ON!

November 12, 1985
Holy Family Hermitage

Dear Father Ed,

Once we've reached a certain goal there can be a tendency to relax and not move on! The author of the Letter to the Hebrews was concerned about this. In the five sections of his letter he exhorts his readers to move on and advance to maturity (e.g. *Heb.* 6:1). And it seems that he is writing to priests! Listen to what he says to us, "God is not unjust; He will not forget your work and the love you have shown Him by your service, past and present, to His holy people." Then he goes on with his exhortation to persevere, "our desire is that each of you show the same zeal till the end..." (*Heb.* 6:10-11).

This same concern to "move on" has been mine for a number of years and now comes back to me with a new force as I reflect over the Letter to the Hebrews, especially, chapters five and six. After ordination we may have had a tendency to slacken off the zeal which initially drove us to move on with the Lord. Or it may be that we've moved on through faithful prayer, retreats, and special graces of the Holy Spirit only to draw back when confronted with a challenge to move on still further. Wherever we are with the Lord we are called to move on: if sitting down, we need to stand firm with Him; if standing still, we need to walk with the Lord; if walking with the Lord, we need to run with Him; and if running with Him, we need to fly!

In working for the renewal of priests my concern these many years has been that we do in fact move beyond the initial experience, whether it be the first conversion, or second or third conversion, etc., or whether it is the initial experience of the baptism in the Holy Spirit. "There is more, there is so much more" (Katherine Kuhlman). And the "more," especially for us priests is sharing in the cross of Christ. The "more" is to move beyond the exclusive focus on conversion from sin and dead works, beyond the exclusively charismatic ministry, beyond the exclusive and inclusive focus on local community to a deeper consecration. This consecration is a total setting aside of everything for the one thing that is set before us: the crucified ministry of Jesus Christ. By moving on by consecration we move beyond the self-concern of self-salvation and self-sanctification and move on to the ministry of salvation and sanctification of others. We move on to the ministry of the Cross, the Cenacle and the fullness of Church.

These three terms have a special meaning to me: The cross is conversion in its fullest, the convergence of grace and history. The cenacle, the upper room, is the place of the full power of the Holy Spirit and the totality of what happened there on Holy Thursday, Easter night, and on Pentecost, namely, the humble washing of one another's feet, the Eucharist, the priestly discourse of Jesus, the reappearance of Jesus, the forgiveness of sin, the intercession for and waiting for the Holy Spirit with Mary and the outpouring of the Holy Spirit—it is the convergence of all the gifts of the Holy Spirit. The Church is the unity of all communities in the unity of all communities, in the unity of the Spirit that Jesus prayed for in the Cenacle under the visible head of Peter.

So this "moving on" is like a pilgrimage up the mountain. By serpentine trails we move up higher and higher. At each new level we can see where we have been, almost in the same place but now hundreds of feet higher! Moving beyond the initial focus on conversion, charisma and community we reach another level of experiencing these things in the cross, in the cenacle, and in the church.

The main point of difference between these two levels of related realities is that the focus is changed—changed from self to others. We move from a concern of our own conversion to the conversion of others by the power of the cross. We move from a use of gifts for our own personal well-being and that of others to a use of the gifts for the building up of the entire Church and for promoting the fulfillment of the kingdom. We move from the forming of local communities for our own mutual support to the strengthening of the unity of the whole church and salvation of the world. This kind of "moving on," this kind of advancing to maturity, means sharing in the redemptive incarnation of Jesus Christ, Who came among us for the salvation of the many.

This kind of "moving on" and advancing to maturity is also a moving from a zeal that expends our human energies, to a radical trust in the Lord. It is a moving on from a focus on planning and programs to coming before the Lord in emptiness and child-like simplicity, seeking His mercy. It is moving to a radical search for the will of the Lord. It involves waiting with patient endurance for the Lord to act.

Where am I in the journey? I've moved into a stage of waiting on the Lord, trying to be faithful to Him. Over the past year I've had this word in my heart and I've tried to respond to it. It has come several times during this time of hermitage: "Be faithful to Me. I am preparing something for you that you do not expect." My response to "be faithful" is to trust the Lord, to be present to Him, as a priority, with joy and thanksgiving. I have no future plans but I do have my heart's desire—to proclaim the Lord's mercy out of a community dedicated to Mary, living a life of intercession with times of solitude. I am waiting on the Lord because at this stage the most needed and precious thing He can do for me is to teach me to live in trust of Him in the arms of Mary, and teach me to know the Father's love and live in that love.

And so, Ed, I'll bring this letter to a conclusion. It is an area of great concern for me, not anxiety, but a longing for moving on with the Lord, a longing for myself and for my brother priests. And I conclude on a very simple note—but the most important: Trust the Lord.

In Jesus our High Priest,
Father George

23. THE PRIEST AS A MAN OF THANKSGIVING

> November 13, 1985
> *Holy Family Hermitage*

Dear Father Ed,

Let us give thanks to the Lord!
In today's liturgy I gave a homily on the text of the day, *Luke* 17:11-19, on the one out of ten lepers that returned to give thanks to the Lord for being cleansed. The preparation of the homily, the giving of the homily and my communion time reflection on the homily were all sources of insight and grace. I came to understand that thanksgiving can be a whole way of life especially for us priests. And so I'm dashing off this letter about thanksgiving, in thanksgiving for the graces received.

While praying in preparation for the homily, I asked for the Lord's desire: "What do You want said to us at this Eucharist?" The one word that summarized the message was to be "Thanksgiving." Then I reflected on the meaning of Thanksgiving. What do we do in giving thanks and what does a "thank you" really mean? Is there more to it than that? I then focused on the fact that we begin thanksgiving with an awareness that a gift has been given and that our focus of thanksgiving should be on the gift given. But I knew there was still more to thanksgiving than the two dimensions of awareness and acknowledgment of the gift and the giver.

For some more information I checked the Webster's Dictionary and J. L. McKenzie's *Dictionary of the Bible* (Bruce, Milwaukee, 1965), the only handy references I had available here in the cell, but I found nothing significant about thanksgiving. So back to prayer, and eureka! A third element of thanksgiving is to return some of the gift in a sign or symbol or "in-turn" to do something with the gift. We can "in-turn" use the gift to honor the giver, for example, our talents can be used and developed to honor God and this is thanksgiving. Tithing is in a sense a thanksgiving because by it we acknowledge that all we have is a gift from God and all belongs to Him and when we give ten percent to those who nourish us in any way we are giving thanks. And so too when we forgive others, we are giving thanks for having been forgiven (the Our Father); when we love others as we have been loved we are giving thanks.

So thanksgiving has three basic elements: awareness, acknowledgment, and a turning (by returning or acting "in-turn"). Thanksgiving then involves thought, word and deed.

Then when I was actually giving the homily I realized that the text itself had these three elements of thanksgiving: The Samaritan leper realized that he was healed, "turned back," acknowledging and praising God with a loud voice. One of the ten returned to give thanks!

We have been healed, forgiven and saved by the mercy of God given in Christ Jesus. And we have a very special way of giving thanks because Jesus Himself became our thanksgiving to the Father for His gift of mercy. Jesus our elder brother returned to the Father, by the way of totally giving Himself in sacrifice. But, thanks be to God, He did this in such a way that we were not left orphans, even though He did indeed return to the Father. He remained with us by the action of the Holy Spirit in the Eucharist, the act of thanksgiving par excellence.

As a priest I can live my life as a life of thanksgiving, I can grow in awareness by living in His presence, listening to Him and coming to know Him as my Father and the Giver of all good gifts. I can acknowledge Him in praise, in preaching, in teaching, in sharing, in writing. I can return the gift in kind by offering daily the gift of His Son, offered with my love and gift of my life. I can "in-turn" use the gifts of mercy and love for others even as I have received mercy and love. Especially as a priest I can dedicate myself to thankfulness (*Col.* 3:15) so that whatever I do, whether in speech or in action I can do it in the name of the Lord Jesus giving thanks to God the Father through Him (*Col.* 3:17).

Thanksgiving has been part of my spiritual armor. The text of *1 Thessalonians* 5:16-18 has been a favorite of mine since high school days: "Rejoice in the Lord always, pray without ceasing, in all things give thanks for this is the will of God in Christ Jesus regarding you all" (Confraternity version). One of the special graces of the thirty day directed Ignation retreat of January-February 1974, was the contemplation on God's love where I wrote down page after page of the things I thanked God for. Thanks be to God for the overwhelming presence of His love that came upon me. Over the years I've found that when I've run out of steam, or am down for some reason or other, an hour of thanksgiving—just listing the things I need to be thankful for—is always a time of special grace, a time of uplifting.

And today, a new facet of thanksgiving—returning the gift given with the gift of myself. In offering the Body and Blood of the Lord in thanksgiving, I too can offer myself in return for His gift of life in Christ Jesus. And the way of giving myself that is most alive in me these days is to be present to the Father as His son in the arms of Mary. To be present to the Father is to be aware of Him; it is to acknowledge Him as the Giver of all good gifts, and it is to return to the Father, like the prodigal son, to return to my healer and savior like the Samaritan leper and to give thanks and praise. To give thanks to the Father is also to trust Him for Who He is—Father and Giver of all good gifts (see *Lk.* 11:13 and *Jas.* 1:17).

"Let us give thanks to the Lord" (preface of every Eucharist).

Fr. George

24. SIN IS THE ISSUE

November 14, 1985
Holy Family Hermitage

Dear Father Ed,

The Merciful Lord be with you.
SIN is the Issue!
Sin is the reason that there is a priesthood. No sin, no priesthood. Sin is the reason Jesus came to save us by His passion, death, and resurrection. And there is plenty of sin in this world that needs "priesting!" The pile of sin like a manure heap is reaching to the heavens—or better, it is reeking to Heaven. How long will God protect us with His merciful hand? How long will the Lord delay in answering the cry of the poor, the orphan and the widow? Almost half the people who ever lived on this planet earth are alive today (some 5 billion of an estimated total of 10 billion) and this means our age has added about half the pile of sin of the world, if not more, with our technologically developed capability of sinning with arms, nuclear weapons, pornography, abortion, birth control, euthanasia, drugs, and economic injustice. How long, oh Lord?

As priests we must face up to the issue of sin—both in our lives and in the world, and proclaim the mercy of Jesus. This is the meaning of our redemption. This is the meaning of our priesthood: the forgiveness of our sins (see *Col.* 1:14). This is the meaning of the cross; this is the meaning of the sacraments of Baptism, Reconciliation, and Eucharist. Christ came to save sinners with His infinite mercy.

The Lord's "blueprint" of what He wants for us is Mary in her Immaculate Conception. His plan is that we share in her grace and be immaculate, free from sin like her. Sin is the great obstacle to our freedom as children of God. Sin prevents us from being what we are and are to be. And yet SIN, bad as it is, is not the greatest evil—there is something worse and that is staying in sin, not turning to the mercy of God. And here is where our priesthood is so powerful—we are vessels of mercy. We can bring people to turn to the mercy of the Lord by our preaching; we can bring sinners to the font of mercy, to the Cross itself, to the crucified Lord pierced for our offenses. We can bring to sinners forgiveness of sin and healing, and new life in the sacraments of life.

And it all begins with me. "I am a sinner; Lord, have mercy." As a sinner, like my fellow sinners, I know I need mercy and so I am a sinful vessel of mercy—a vessel of clay, cracked and leaky, but nonetheless a vessel of mercy. This past year one of the special graces for me has been the increasing awareness of my sinfulness—not that I am blatantly breaking more of the commandments, but that I have squandered so many of God's graces. Again this past week I was led in prayer to repent of the sins of my whole life. Category after category came to mind as, convicted by the Spirit, I repented for each incident as it came up before my mind's eye: "I repent, Lord have mercy on me and those involved."

Another grace, recently received, has been the increasing awareness of the Lord's faithfulness to me over the years, reaching out to me when I was about to take a wrong step, keeping after me when I was walking in the dark, turning me around when I went down the wrong path, sheltering me from sin and danger when I was not aware of it at the time. And the sin in all this is that I have not been aware of it to thank Him and in turn do something about it!

A teaching given by Father Jim Henderson, O.C.S.O., the trappist who was with us on the team at Bethany House of Intercession, has come back with new force. Jim gave a teaching on Father F. Faber's search for the fundamental attitude of a true Christian. After searching for many years, and setting aside many good and noble attitudes, Father Faber came up with this as the basic attitude: "The abiding compunction for sin." This may sound negative but it really isn't. It is a peaceful and joyful realization that I am a sinner—in fact, I'm a great one, because I have received so many great graces and have not cooperated with them, at least to the extent that I should have. And at the same time this "abiding compunction" is a continual "prick" or "sting" from the Holy Spirit to turn to the abiding and infinite mercy of God.

This gives me a better appreciation of the spirituality of the eastern monks who live the Jesus Prayer, breathing it throughout the day: "Jesus, Son of God, have mercy on me a sinner." As I am cleansed of my sin by the mercy of God, then I become a more effective instrument and vessel of mercy for others. I can then cry out, "Lord, have mercy on us and on the whole world."

I found it helpful to review the text of the Mass and remind myself of the many, many times that forgiveness of sin and mercy come into the liturgy: the penitential rite with the Kyrie and prayer, the Gloria, the gospel response of the priest, the Creed, the offertory prayer, the words of consecration and Canon, the Lord's prayer, the Deliver us prayer, the prayer for peace, Lamb of God, the communion preparation, the Lord I am not worthy, the purification prayers, as well as the orations and readings which are so regularly messages of mercy for sinners.

Between the celebration of the Eucharist, of the Sacrament of Reconciliation, and the ministry of preaching on the Lord's mercy, we can be full-time vessels of mercy! How many times the cry for mercy occurs in the psalms and readings of the daily Liturgy of the Hours. How many times we pray to Mary in the rosary: ". . . pray for us sinners now and at the hour of our death." Not a bad idea—"full-time vessels of mercy"—a whole way of life for us as priests.

Yes, sin is the issue, but mercy is the answer. The Lord has ordained us to be men with the answer—the mercy of our Lord Jesus Christ.

In His mercy,
Fr. George

25. THE PRESENCE OF THE PRIEST AS EUCHARIST

November 16, 1985
Holy Family Hermitage

Dear Father Ed,

For some time I've wanted to write to you about the Eucharist, but it hasn't been the right moment until now. I've been waiting for the anointing of something special to share with you. Earlier this morning in prayer before the Blessed Sacrament I asked the Lord for such a special anointing so that I could be aware of Him in a new and deeper way. And immediately the answer came in one word, "presence." As I pondered His presence I was flooded with the various ways He was present in the Eucharist. After a while I sat down and wrote out these ways of presence like a litany. The first one that started off my prayer was: "You are the Holy One, You are the Humble One, You are the Merciful One." But in writing it out I started out with His presence in the Eucharist.

JESUS, YOU ARE PRESENT!

(The RESPONSE is:—*Jesus, You are present!*)

Jesus, You are here in the Eucharist—
As Son of the Father and Son of Mary (Creed)—
As at the Annunciation when You, the Word, were made flesh (*Lk.* 1; *Jn.* 1)—
By word and the Spirit (*Jn.* 3)—
As Mercy Incarnate (John Paul II)—
Because You love us (*Jn.* 13:11)—

As the Lamb of God (*Jn.* 1:29)—
As totally given and poured out (*Lk.* 22:19-20)—
As the New Covenant (*Jn.* 6:27, *Lk.* 22:20)—
Body and Blood, Soul and Divinity (Council of Trent)—
As the Memorial of Your passion, death and resurrection (Canon of Mass)—
As the remembrance of all You have done for us (*1 Cor.* 11:25)—
As the thanksgiving to the Father (*Mt.* 26:27)—
As the sacrificial Gift to the Father (*Heb.* 10:10)—
As the Promise of resurrection (see *1 Cor.* 11:30)—
To give us eternal life (*Jn.* 6:51-58)—
To nourish us (*Jn.* 6:54)—
As "My Lord and my God," (*Jn.* 20:28)—
As the Icon of the invisible God (*Col.* 1:15)—
Though hidden like the Father—
As a Pleasing Aroma to the Father (see *2 Cor.* 2:15)—
As Priest, Prophet and King—
As the Holy One, the Humble One, the Merciful One—
In all past and future (O Sacrum convivium)—
As the pledge of Your coming again (see *1 Cor.* 11:26)—
As the Bridegroom longing for communion (*Lk.* 22:15)—
As the Mystery of Faith—
As the Mystery of Mercy—
As the Hope of Glory—
Jesus, You are here and You call us (*Jn.* 11:28)—

This litany of **presence** was an eye-opener for me. I saw that **presence** is a unifying concept of the Eucharist. The passion, death, and resurrection of Jesus Christ our Lord are a sacrifice because they are sacramentally **present** (theology of Father Vonier); the divinization of man is brought about by the communion of our mutual **presence**. Through the **presence** of the resurrected and glorified Lord we give all honor and glory to the Father. Through the Lord's **presence** in me by the Eucharist He can be **present** to the world—He is **present** in me that I might be witness to Him to others. His **presence** among us in the Eucharist is the ultimate gift of love and humility—He entrusted Himself to our hands. He not only gave Himself for our salvation on the cross but He continues to give us Himself as our food for eternal life as well.

This litany of *presence* was a review of the theology and spirituality of the Eucharist. And over and above that, it was for me a summary of the main graces of this sabbatical of solitude up to this present time.

How strong and beautiful are those words of the Third Eucharistic Prayer: "Grant that we, who are nourished by His body and blood, may be filled with His Holy Spirit, and become one body, one spirit in Christ."

"Vatican II on the Liturgy" clearly stated the Church's teaching on the most sacred mystery of the Eucharist:

> At the Last Supper, on the night He was betrayed, Our Savior instituted the Eucharistic Sacrifice of His Body and Blood. He did this in order to perpetuate the Sacrifice of the Cross throughout the centuries until He should come again, and so to entrust to His beloved spouse, the Church, a memorial of His death and resurrection: a sacrament of love, a sign of unity, a hand of charity (St. Augustine), a paschal banquet in which Christ is consumed, the mind is filled with grace, and a pledge of future glory is given to us" (*O Sacrum convivium,* second vespers, Feast of Corpus Christi, St. Thomas Aquinas) (*Sacrosanctum Concilium, #47*).

John Paul II in his first encyclical "Redemptor Hominis," #20, develops the meaning of the Eucharist—

> It is the life of the Church...With all the greater reason, then, it is not permissible for us, in thought, life or action, to take away from this truly most holy Sacrament its full magnitude and its essential meaning. It is at one and the same time a Sacrifice-Sacrament, a Communion-Sacrament, and a Presence-Sacrament.

To grasp the "full magnitude and its essential meaning" all three dimensions of the Eucharist must be there—not just one or the other. Haven't we become weak on the sacrificial dimension and on the presence dimension because of our great stress in these recent years on the communion and fellowship dimension? It's a question worth pondering.

Conchita (Concepcion Cabrera de Armida): Under the guidance of her spiritual directors, seven in all, (and her last spiritual director (1925-1937) was the Archbishop-primate of Mexico, Msgr. Luis Maria Martinez (1881-1956), Conchita, a Mexican housewife and mystic, wrote down what the Lord "dictated" to her over a fifty-year period. The Lord instructed her on the great spiritual themes of the cross, Mary, the Church, the Holy Spirit, and the priesthood. Her writings on Eucharist and priesthood have been the inspiration of much of my current thinking. Here is just one paragraph on the priest and the Eucharist, just one to whet your appetite so that you might get the book and read more! Jesus is speaking to Conchita:

> My Father wants to see the priest transformed into Me, not only during the time of Mass, but at all times. He wants to see him transformed in such a way that no matter where or when, the priest can say, in the interior of his soul, these blessed words, constantly fulfilled in him by his transformation into Me: *This is my Body; This is my Blood* (Diary, Dec. 31, 1927, quoted in *Conchita: A Mother's Spiritual Diary,* edited by M.M. Philipon, O.P., Alba House, NY 10314, 1978, p. 202).

Father Philipon comments on this section of transformation into Christ-Victim; "Transformation into Christ demands being with Him at the same time as priest and victim. The grandeur of the priest is essentially a eucharistic grandeur" (p. 203). The sacrificial dimension of Eucharist is essential.

Conchita repeatedly conveys the Lord's teaching that it is by the Holy Spirit that we are transformed. It is the Holy Spirit that makes us the Body and Blood of the Lord to be given and poured out for the redemption of the world. It is the Holy Spirit who will revitalize the priests and through the priests revitalize the church. The Lord wants to renew the world by being present to the world through His priests. But this means holy priests, priests sanctified by the Holy

Spirit—priests who have become Eucharist to the world. It is through the united action of the Holy Spirit and Mary that we are formed into the living Eucharist present to the world.

After jotting down a few of Conchita's themes on the priesthood and Eucharist I've resolved to read the book a fourth time! I haven't read it since I began my time in solitude. I can see that it will mean so much more.

May the Holy Spirit form you in the Heart of Mary to have the Eucharistic Heart of Jesus, and bring His mercy to the world.

Fr. George

26. HASTENING THE DAY OF THE LORD

November 19, 1985
Holy Family Hermitage

Dear Father Ed,

Today I'm conscious of the need to implore the Lord for His mercy and to beseech Him to send His Holy Spirit. Several things converge to increase this consciousness in me. Sunday we read in the Liturgy of the coming of the Lord. We are approaching the third millenium, the increasing tension in the world situation, the continued catastrophes of nature, and particularly today the summit meeting of the president of the United States and the premier of the Soviet Union. Today we offered the Eucharist in honor of the Holy Spirit for the intention of this meeting.

In the homily I preached on the gospel of *John* 20, where Jesus appeared in the cenacle on Easter Sunday night. I really preached a word that I needed to hear—like so often, the first one who needs the word preached is the preacher himself. Jesus came into the upper room in victory, passing through the locked doors, radiant in His victory over death, risen with His glorious wounds visible as trophies, entering as the High Priest coming out of the Holy of Holies with treasures of victory—Peace, authority, the Holy Spirit and Forgiveness of sin; in a word—mercy! Only the victorious coming of Jesus can possibly bring us peace! He alone is the source of that peace which the world cannot give. No president, no premier can give us real peace. Only Jesus can give us His Holy Spirit to purify us and change our hearts. Only Jesus can give us the authority to forgive sins. Only the Mercy of God that forgives sin can take away this real obstacle to peace.

However, it is necessary that we implore the Holy Spirit to come and flood us with mercy, especially the leaders, the president and the premier, and "the kings and those in authority that we may live tranquil lives in perfect piety and dignity" (*1 Tim.* 2:2). These leaders are in a position to remove the obstacles to living in peace. They need our support and prayer of intercession.

One such prayer the church has been praying for centuries is the "Come, Holy Ghost." We need to pray it with greater expectant faith.

Another prayer we need to pray with greater perseverance and expectancy is the prayer of the Church: "Come, Lord Jesus!" In this past Sunday's liturgy I found a clue to what is holding up and delaying the coming of the Lord! I consider it a very significant clue to forming our whole attitude toward the coming of the Lord. As the gospel of Sunday said, we don't know the day or the hour—no one but the Father knows it (see *Mk.* 13:32)—but there is something we do know and we profess it as our faith and that is the fact that He is coming. We do not know when but we do know that He is coming again.

But He is waiting. Waiting for what and for whom? The reading from Hebrews puts it this way: "But Jesus offered one sacrifice for sins and took His seat forever at the right hand of God: now He waits until His enemies are placed beneath His feet" (*Heb.* 10:13). Jesus is waiting for us to put His enemies beneath His feet. This is the clue that led to other clues. Like Sherlock Holmes we can put them in juxtaposition and draw some conclusions on how to hasten the day of the Lord. If we do our part the Lord will not need to wait so long!

We can hasten the coming of the Lord, because Jesus has given us, the Church, the role of participating in His redemptive incarnation. We are to crush the head of Satan, and place Him at the feet of Jesus, with our humility, our obedience and submission. Jesus is waiting for us. We can hasten the day of His coming by fulfilling our part. St. Peter tells us of other ways to hasten the day of the Lord: by our holiness (*2 Ptr.* 3:11-12) and by our repentance (*2 Ptr.* 3:9) so that God can have mercy on all! So again we see the importance of the triplet: Be holy, Be humble, Be merciful—and so hasten the day of the Lord!

Another clue to hastening the day of the Lord comes from St. Paul's Letter to the Corinthians in which he deals with the celebration of the Eucharist. "Every time you eat this bread and drink this cup, you proclaim the death of the Lord until He comes! (*1 Cor.* 11:26)—also used in the proclamation of the Mass. The clue focuses on the word "until." Joachim Jeremiah (in *Eucharistic Words of Jesus*) points out that "until" besides meaning "a time when," can also have the meaning of purpose. So "we proclaim the death of the Lord in order that He come." This means that each time we offer the Eucharist we hasten the day of the Lord. The Lord is waiting for us priests to offer the Eucharist with that intention! Come, Lord Jesus, come in glory.

Again in the letter to the Corinthians St. Paul gives another clue to the reason for the delay in the Lord's coming: "Christ must reign until God has put all enemies under His feet, and the last enemy to be destroyed is death" (*1 Cor.* 15:25-26).

So the Lord is waiting until all His enemies—sin, Satan and death—are defeated in me and in as many as possible that He might have mercy on all (*Rom.* 11:32). He is showing "generous patience since He wants none to perish but all to come to repentance" (*2 Ptr.* 3:9). Like the farmer in charge of the fruitless fig tree He asks for another year to save a few more souls, and another year and another. And so, almost 2,000 years have gone by! How long will the Lord wait for us? Especially for us priests?

The Lord is showing generous patience! And yet all the signs of the times indicate that He is coming to the end of His patience. I have a personal interpretation of when the Lord will come, not a date nor a year, but the condition for His coming. When enough holy people cry out with expectant faith, "Come, Lord Jesus!" He will be here!

It seems that it almost happened a number of times through the 2,000 years, but each time we blew it by our sinful actions: becoming attached to the Roman Empire, dividing the Church into East and West, conducting Crusades against fellow Christians, Reformation by division, enthroning of reason, the cult of man by secularism. It would be interesting for a historian to correlate the periods of special holiness of the people and the times of greater sin and corruption with this personal theory of the Lord's coming. For sure, the Lord has been waiting for us to be a holy people ready to welcome Him.

He wants us to live like the five prudent virgins with lamps lit and oil in reserve, ready to greet the bridegroom on His return.

Pope John Paul II seems to have some special insight into the turn of the century. Some five times in his first encyclical, "Redeemer of Man" and on a number of occasions he has referred to the year 2,000 as a "New Advent"—a new coming, with a mystical sense. Again I have a personal interpretation of the year 2,000. St. Peter speaks of the Lord's timing, "In the Lord's eyes, one day is as a thousand years and a thousand years are as a day" (*2 Ptr.* 3:8). So, if we are approaching the year 2,000, it is like the beginning of the third day; it is like the beginning of the day of resurrection! It could be the day of the Lord's appearing with His victory trophies of peace, authority, the Holy Spirit and mercy! The author of the letter to the Hebrews tells us: "He will appear a second time, not to take away sin but to bring salvation to those who eagerly await Him" (*Heb.* 9:28). He is coming again with His mercy for all who await Him.

As priests we have a special charge to prepare the people for His coming. It is more urgent than ever. The Lord doesn't want anyone to perish and has placed us in the responsible position of preparing the people. If our people perish, we perish with them! The time is urgent. Now is the time for mercy and preparation by holiness, humility and our imploring Him by offering the death of the Lord until He comes in glory.

Come, Holy Spirit, prepare the hearts of the faithful.
Come, Lord Jesus!

Fr. George

27. DIVISION OF EAST AND WEST

November 20, 1985
Holy Family Hermitage

Dear Father Ed,

The division between the Eastern and Western Church is on my heart. I think it's a major scandal and an obstacle to effective world evangelization. If Christians cannot be one, then who can be? The need to seriously intercede for Church unity was awakened by the visit of Archbishop Tawil to the hermitage. Archbishop Joseph Tawil, as the bishop of the Melkites in the United States, has come to honor the Melkite monks in Steubenville on the occasion of the fifteenth year of their foundation. They all came out here on Sunday because of friendship with Fr. Charles. We had a grand celebration of the Divine Liturgy with the monks (four of them) singing, the Archbishop presiding. The deacon, Brother Philaret, Superior of the monks, sang with a magnificent voice and used great quantities of incense—all to my delight! I felt right at home again. For two years, at Bethany House of Intercession, Father Seraphim Michalenko celebrated the byzantine liturgy for us, with the same Melkite hymns. I received the Body and Blood of the Lord from the hands of the Archbishop.

After the Liturgy I shared with the Archbishop about our mutual friend, Father Seraphim and his work on the Divine Mercy. The Archbishop said that the devotion fits right into the eastern devotion of the Divine Compassion. Then I asked him how I would get permission to celebrate in the byzantine rite. He said, "Get a letter from your Superior General and write to me and I'll give it to you!" It would be an answer to my prayer from our first intercessory program of prayer in 1974. I publicly prayed for the faculties needed to celebrate the byzantine liturgy in order to intercede for church unity.

At the dinner that followed in honor of Archbishop Tawil, he said several things that stirred my longing for unity of East and West. When working in Damascus with some of the Greek Orthodox bishops along with the Greek Catholic Patriarch, the question came up as to who would be patriarch if there were union. The Melkite's answer was one of great humility: "We would resign and you would be the patriarch." When working with the Syrian bishop in trying to form a common catechism, the issue of the two natures and one person of Christ came to the fore. This was the issue that the Syrians did not accept at the Council of Chalcedon. Archbishop Tawil asked in response to their concern three questions:

1) "Do you believe Jesus Christ is True Man?" "Yes," they replied.
2) "Do you believe that Jesus Christ is True God?" "Yes," they replied.
3) "Do you believe that Jesus Christ is one?" "Yes," they replied. "Then that's what we'll say in the Catechism. That is our faith too. We don't need to use the Greek philosophical terms of nature and person that caused the division."

Further, Archbishop Tawil expressed his hope to us that the union wouldn't come too quickly because the people on both sides need to be prepared. He also said that in his recent visit with Pope John Paul II he congratulated the Holy Father on his ecumenical work and his support of Lebanon. He also said to the Pope that the eastern bishops read very carefully his statements on unity of East and West. I asked the Archbishop what the effect has been of John Paul II's Encyclical on Sts. Cyril and Methodius. He said that it awakened the Church to the fact that the Slavs are an integral part of the European Church.

I shared with him an example of the division that politics caused in my own family. My great grandmother had two sons lost in Siberia and a third son at home at the time of the 1863 Polish uprising against Russia. She went to confession and the priest asked her if she had any sons. She said, "I have one twelve-year-old at home." The priest said, "He should be in the uprising or I won't give you absolution!" She walked out of the confessional and out of the Church and joined the Lutheran Church along with her third son, my maternal grandfather who remained a Lutheran. Politics, language, philosophical terms, cultural differences, and party spirits have often become a work of the evil one that has kept the Churches divided! Lord, forgive us for tearing apart Your seamless garment. The Roman soldiers didn't do it; but we tore it apart by our sins and the sins of the world.

Archbishop Tawil responded with an historical example of politics that caused the division of East and West. It was the issue of the crowning by the Pope of the Emperor Charlemagne. The eastern church said, "That's it! They've gone their own way!" The church was divided—emperors ruling the church and popes ruling the empire, and that in both East and West.

Father Charles pointed out the fascinating fact that the brothers Sts. Cyril and Methodius came from the eastern church into the area now called Moravia and established the roots of what was later the Polish Church, a Roman Latin-Rite church just prior to the terrible division. St. Methodius is buried some thirty miles across the border from Father Charles' home town in Poland and St. Cyril is buried in St. Clement's Church in Rome.

There are a number of other incidents in my life that fit together like pieces of a mosaic yet to be finished, that make me sensitive to the division of the East and the West. The fact that I am Polish, and Mother and Dad were born and raised in Czarist Russia, for instance. My visit to Russia as a biochemist in 1961 gave me the opportunity to visit some of my roots. I attended liturgies in Russian Churches in Moscow and Zargorsk, and visited Archbishop Nichodeem, the Metropolitan who suffered a heart attack in the arms of Pope John Paul I. I asked the Archbishop about church unity and he responded, "It will take much love!"

This summer I visited Father Murray Bogdasavitch, the hermit living in conjunction with Madonna House, Combermere, Ontario. Murray is a fellow Basilian, now a Byzantine hermit living the Mount Athos style of eremitical life. After a warm greeting he confronted me. "Why aren't you doing something in writing, talking, praying about the unity of East and West. We are both in sin and we are both incomplete without each other!" May this letter be the beginning of a little response.

In May of 1981, just a week prior to his being shot, Pope John Paul II addressed the delegates of the International Leaders Conference of the Charismatic Renewal, held in Rome, and said to them that they had a special gift for ecumenism, and that they should pray that the Holy Spirit reveal His strategy for unity. The unity of East and West continues to be a major thrust of Pope John Paul II's Pontificate. He has acted boldly and with anointing in establishing a mutual commission of study. He spoke of the Church needing East and West like needing the two lungs we breathe with.

One strategy for Church Unity I heard from Pastor Larry Christensen, a Lutheran pastor in California. A woman in his parish reported a vision she had of a tremendous logjam that blocked the flow of the river. She looked at the logs and noticed various labels on them—Lutheran, Catholic, Orthodox, etc. She then asked the Lord to help with this logjam of Church dis-unity. She pleaded, "Do something, Lord, to free us!" The Lord responded, "I could blow the logjam sky high!" "Oh, no, Lord," she replied, "that is not Your way! What is Your way, Lord?" The Lord answered, "My way is to ask you to ask Me to raise the level of the water!" The Lord's way is to increase the flow of living water as we intercede! As the water level rises and the Spirit floods us, we will be freed from the logjam and the river will flow. That is God's strategy—more outpouring of the Holy Spirit. Our part is to intercede for church unity by asking for the outpouring of the Spirit.

Our part is to intercede. It is a simple role we are given, but because of its simplicity we can turn away with the attitude of Naaman: it's just too simple to wash seven times in the Jordan! (see *2 Kgs.* 5:1-27). We have a magnificent advantage in praying for Church unity, namely, the fact that Jesus prayed for it on the night before He died. After praying for His disciples He prayed:

I pray also for those who will believe in Me through their word, ***that all may be one*** as You, Father, are in Me, and I in You.'' (*Jn.* 17:20-21). Jesus prayed for unity and that prayer will be answered! We will be one—so that the world may know that Jesus was sent by the Father (see *Jn.* 17:23).

During this hermitage time, I am growing in the awareness of the need of intercession—with the simple cry of the heart:

>Come, Holy Spirit
>Come, Lord Jesus.
>Have mercy on us.
>Make us one! That the world may know that You are its Lord and Savior.

>>Let us continue to pray
>>for the Holy Spirit to come,
>>Fr. George

28. THE MARIAN MOVEMENT OF PRIESTS

November 21, 1985
Holy Family Hermitage

Dear Father Ed,

Today is the Feast of the Presentation of our Lady. It is the 163rd birthday of the Basilian Fathers and a day of renewing of vows for many communities. In early morning prayer time I was moved to make the topic of today's letter The Marian Movement of Priests. It is a sensitive topic for some priests so I want to approach it by way of my own experience over these eight years of involvement with the movement. I'll list the problems and questions I've encountered and then try to give some light on the issues with the hope that some of the obstacles will be removed and a few questions and problems clarified. I can't convince anyone by argumentation, nor do I intend to, but the grace of God may use some of these reflections to help a brother priest in his relationship with Mary and with the words in the book *Our Lady Speaks to Her Beloved Priests,* (The Marian Movement of Priests, Milan; 8th English edition, P.O. Box 8, St. Francis, ME 04774).

The Marian Movement of Priests is important in my life and has had a very significant influence on my thinking, preaching and writing as well as on my spiritual life. I've faithfully read and re-read the book over and over again during the last eight years. Each day there is some special word to feed me and form me. Since it is so significant, especially during this time of solitude, I want to respond to concerns that I myself have had and also to the concerns others have voiced to me. Precisely because it is a sensitive and even divisive topic I want to deal with it as forthrightly as I can.

But, beyond my personal reasons for dealing with this movement, the messages themselves are reason enough to study the book. The words reported from Mary are of the utmost importance for our salvation and the salvation of souls. These are urgent times and they call for a very special response. I feel that the Lord is speaking to us through His mother in order that we priests be aware and be prepared for the difficult times ahead. We as shepherds are responsible for the flock, especially in times of difficulty and attack. And we are in times of great difficulty; we are under attack.

In listing these questions and problems I obviously won't use the names of those involved but they sure would make a fascinating list of Who's Who in the Church:

1. Who is this Gobbi fellow, anyway? We're just getting a rehash of his traditional piety.
2. It turns me off when I see the type of priests involved—old timers, ultra-conservatives, those not up-to-date with Vatican II or the current theology. They're just reactionaries.
3. The saccharine sentimentality and piety in the book turns me off. That's not for me.
4. From reading some of the book I find that Mary wants me to have a personal relationship with her like I have with Jesus. She is placing herself in the place of Jesus.
5. The message is all right but the strategy and timing are not right.
6. The message is a construct of piety that goes beyond reason and beyond what scholars have shown us is in the sacred scriptures.
7. Marian devotion is a private matter and it's optional. This is not for me.
8. Private revelations and locutions are not a matter of faith and morals. There is enough for me in the scriptures and in the official teaching of the Church. I don't need private revelations.
9. Mary talks to us as though we are children. I don't like it.
10. The content of the message is too apocalyptic. Too much threat of end times.

Ten concerns may be enough for one letter. There may be other concerns but I think this covers the main ground. As

I said, don't expect a theological treatise, but hopefully some insights from my experience and readings can help:

1. Don Stefano Gobbi is a priest from Milan, Italy, and has been recording the locutions he has received from Mary in a book called *Our Lady Speaks to Her Beloved Priests* now in its eighth edition in English (almost 500 pages with introduction and index). I've had the opportunity to meet Father Gobbi and to hear him speak publicly and privately on three different occasions. This dark, short, tubby and very jovial man reminded me of what Pope John XXIII might have looked like in his late forties. His simplicity and joy impressed me.

   The locutions he receives are submitted to his spiritual director who clears them for publication. The current edition has the imprimatur of Archbishop Byrne of Dubuque. The Italian edition has been cleared by Archbishop Martini of Milan.

   Stefano Gobbi asked our Lady why she chose him. He got back a very supportive response! She responded to him:

   > You ask Me why I have chosen you to spread my movement while you feel so inadequate and helpless. Rightly do you see your nothingness and weaknesses and you ask Me: "Why do you not choose someone more suitable and capable than me? How can you rely on me when you know very well my past infidelities?" My Son, I have chosen you because you are the least apt instrument; thus no one will say that this is your work. The Marian Movement of Priests must be my work alone. Through your weakness I will manifest my strength; through your nothingness I will manifest my power (*Our Lady Speaks to Her Beloved Priests,* July 16, 1973).

   I heard Don Gobbi quote this a number of times: "I'm the least apt instrument Mary could find!" His joy and good humor are infectious.

   While waiting for one of his talks to start, I turned to Father John Randall of Providence, RI, and said, "We need to find a way to stay on the sharp edge of orthodoxy and orthopraxis, without going to the extremes of liberalism or conservatism." Immediately Father Gobbi started his talk with, "If you want to stay on the sharp edge of the balance between progressivism and traditionalism, then consecrate yourselves to Mary; she'll take you to the heart of the Church." I gulped in amazement and paid close attention to the rest of the talk.

2. I, too, was really concerned about the type of following the presence of Dob Gobbi would attract when Father Albert Roux phoned me in the late winter of 1978, and asked if Bethany House of Intercession would organize a Conference-Retreat for priests of the Marian Movement. He estimated that fifty priests at the most would come to hear Father Gobbi for a three day retreat. It turned out that one hundred twenty priests came, and my expectation of what type of priest would show up was far exceeded! I've never run across such a bunch of complainers! They had my secretary in tears with their demands and complaints. What impressed me, however, is how they changed in three days. Into the end of the first day, Stefano Gobbi was leading the second rosary and suddenly stopped in the middle of its recitation and said to us: "You're not praying. You're rattling off the rosary. Now, let's start praying!" With that the mood started to change! By the end of the second day the men were meek as lambs and joyful. If he could do that with such a bunch of priests by simply praying the full rosary and giving three simple talks a day, he's got something.

Yes, the Marian Movement of Priests does attract the old, the infirm, the little ones. It seems that these are the ones our Lady wants to use. Yes, the movement attracts those who are strong on Marian devotions and apparitions, including those who we might be tempted to judge as overly involved. Our Lady challenges these men to a deeper commitment and holiness through deeper prayer, silence, suffering and, above all, trust.

3. The question of a saccharine piety and style of the book may be a question of which colored glasses we are reading with. If I read with my academic, rational, intellectual glasses and analyze the words with my mind, I won't read

very much before I put it aside. If, however, I put on glasses that allow my heart to listen, a new light penetrates. It is a word to the heart and it is not a theological discourse. Not that the theology is incorrect; it is just different.

Actually, the style is probably what we really need in order to counteract the overly rationalized theory and spirituality of our times.

4. Yes, Mary does want to have a personal relationship with us. She is our mother! And she cares about us and wants to care for us more, if we allow her. This is one of the key teachings of our Lady—"that ***she really is our mother.***" She is our mother by God's design and choice. I don't need to choose her, that has already been done by God a long time ago.

   Mary's unique role is to form us into the image of Jesus by the power of the Holy Spirit—into another "Jesus." This is the one thing Mary does as Mother—she forms us into Jesus.

   > Do not be afraid of entrusting yourselves completely to Me. I am His mother and yours and I know how to do only one thing for you, and that is to help you to be born and to grow up like other little Jesuses for the salvation of all my children (August 7, 1976).
   >
   > I will make you living copies of my Son Jesus (October 18, 1975).
   >
   > The Priests are children whom I love in a special way because, by their vocation, they are called to be Jesus. It is my duty to form the image of my Son in them (February 23, 1974).

   Mary and the Spirit united give us Jesus, only Jesus, and Jesus only.

5. Mary's message is one of urgency to priests because it is through priests that she will accomplish the renewal of the Church entrusted to her. The designs and plans for us and the renewal of the Church are beyond our strategies and timing:

It is Jesus Whom I want to make live again in these Priests who are consecrated to me, these Priests of my Movement. It is Jesus living in these Priests of mine who will again save my Church at the very moment when it seems to be sinking. If you only knew, my sons, the designs which I have upon you: you would leap for joy! This is why I say to you: Give yourselves to me completely, your whole Priesthood, without fear. Abandon yourselves to me... (June 8, 1974).

It is you, O Priests, sons of my predilection, who are the strategic elements of this plan. My plan can be carried out only through you. Nevertheless, it is not for you to know in detail. It is enough that it is known by Me, as I am your leader (April 29, 1977).

6. The message of our Lady is so simple that it can baffle the scholar. It is simply the gospel lived in its radical simplicity:

> I need only your trust, I want only your complete abandonment to Me (July 29, 1975).
>
> Rely on Me and not on human means; entrust yourself only to Me. There is one thing that you can always do, and which is the only thing that I want you to do at each moment, because it is so useful to me for the Movement: your prayer, your suffering, your trust in Me (February 10, 1974).
>
> Of you, my dearest son, I ask prayer, suffering, and silence (August 5, 1975).

At Bethany House we had an in-house code. When things were tough we'd say "PSST," which stands for our response of: Prayer, Suffering, Silence and Trust.

> The only thing that matters is that you let yourself be formed by Me: for this it is necessary that each one of you offer himself and consecrate himself to My Immaculate Heart and entrust himself to Me as Jesus entrusted Himself totally to Me; and then I will take care of everything. I will form you to a great love for the

> Pope and for the Church united to him. I will prepare you for a heroic witnessing to the Gospel which, for some, will be even to the shedding of their blood (July 16, 1973).

The message is simple, yet simply total in its commitment.

7. Yes, Marian devotion is private and it is personal but it is also public and communal. It is no longer optional because of God's choice of Mary to place her in an integral role in the redemptive incarnation:

   > Do you see how God entrusted Himself completely to this human creature of His? The reason is to be found in the mystery of the Love of God. What moved God to stoop down to Me was the profound sense I had of my littleness and of my poverty, as well as my perfect availability for the accomplishment of the Will of the Lord. God could have chosen many other ways to come to you: but He chose to select mine. And therefore, this way now becomes necessary for you to reach God (March 25, 1976).

   Now, Mary is not an option! Mary is a necessity!

8. In regard to private revelation—God has not stopped speaking to His people with the death of the last apostle, John the beloved disciple. Public revelation was completed with John's death but God continues to speak today and give us assurance of His victory. But the question is: Who is listening?

   Especially in this time of travail, like ours, we need the word of the Lord to be proclaimed clearly and forcefully.

   Here are some reasons I've found helped me to appreciate the word of private revelations more fully:

   - They remind me that God is free—He can speak to us if He wants. God has something important to say to us.
   - They are historical facts.
   - They confirm the Gospel.
   - They give a current emphasis to truths of faith and morals.

- They give guidance and point out a path in times of crises.
- The content of their message contributes to the up-building of our faith.

9. Mary talks to us as she would to children because that is what we are supposed to be! The trouble with not liking it is with us, not with Mary. The gospel message is clear: "Let the children come to Me and do not hinder them. It is to just such as these that the kingdom of God belongs. I assure you that whoever does not accept the reign of God like a little child shall not take part in it" (*Mk.* 10:14-15).

Mary's word on being a child is explained in terms of the current spiritual warfare:

> Walk in simplicity. I am leading you by the hand and you follow me always. Let yourself be led by Me; let yourself be nourished by and cradled by Me; like a little child in My arms.
>
> Since Satan has today deceived the greater part of humanity by pride and by the spirit of rebellion against God, it is only through humility and littleness that it can now encounter and look upon the Lord...
>
> You must return today to simplicity and humility, to the confidence of little children, in order to see God. For this I myself am preparing this cohort: my Priests, whom I will cause to become more little, so that they may be filled with light and the love of God.
>
> Humble, small, abandoned and trusting. they will all let themselves be led by me. Their weak voice will one day be changed into the roar of a hurricane and, joining the victorious cry of the angels, it will resound in a powerful cry throughout the world: "Who is like God? Who is like God?"
>
> Then will come the conclusive defeat of the proud, and my triumph and that of my children (July 24, 1974).

10. Yes, the message is apocalyptic and it deals with the end times because that is the nature of our times! Like a good mother, she wants none of her children lost.

In a sense, the message of our Lady is the message of Fatima but addressed to priests. And Fatima is a message that has the endorsement of the Church, especially by the presence and words of Pope Paul VI and John Paul II.

Our times are like going down the upper Niagara River in a raft. The roar of the falls is getting louder and louder. The urgency of this mesage of our Lady is like a warning cry: "Don't you hear the roar of the falls? Do something now! Take shelter at the shore before it's too late."

May Mary, our mother, form you more and more into the living icon of her merciful Son Jesus.

Fr. George

29. WE NEED A MARRIED PRIESTHOOD
[i.e., Married to the Lord!]

November 22, 1985
Holy Family Hermitage

Dear Father Ed,

We need a married priesthood! How do you like that for a title to stir a little controversy? We need priests who are married to the Lord! "The Lord God said: 'It is not good for the man to be alone. I will make a suitable partner for him" (*Gen.* 2:18). So if we're not married to a woman, then we must be married to the Lord Jesus. The Father has provided a partner that is more than suitable. It is not good for a man to be alone. Granted that the introductory statement is a play on words, the point is that we need priests who are totally given to the Lord, living in union with Him.

Today is the feast of St. Cecilia, virgin and martyr. The early Church rejoiced at the example of such a saint who gave herself without reserve in body, mind, will and heart. Today we need more examples of that kind. I'm drawn toward that kind of life. Would that by the grace of God I could live it.

I'm growing in the awareness that only union with Christ can supply all my needs. Marriage to a wife can't supply all needs; friends and food can't do that either. During the week I've been reading *The Life of Christ* by Nicholas Cabasilas (St. Vladimir's Seminary Press, Crestwood, NY 10707, 1974) who was a 14th Century Byzantine theologian and mystic. Cabasilas' thesis is that Christ alone is man's true life. In one section he writes of our union with Christ as all-sufficient. There are many things we need such as air, food, light, clothing, our natural faculties and members. Yet we do not need each of them constantly for all purposes. "But the Savior is ever present in such a way, in every fashion with those who dwell in Him, that *He supplies their every need* and is all things to them, nor does He suffer them to look to anything else whatever nor seek anything from elsewhere. There is nothing of which the saints are in need which He is not Himself. He gives them birth, growth and nourishment; He is life and breath..." (p. 47).

Our union with Christ is a great mystery (*Eph.* 5:32); it is the model for marriage of man and wife; it is a union of bride and bridegroom, yet it is virginal and total; it is a relation of such intimacy that we are mother, brother, and sister to the Lord Jesus (*Mk.* 3:31-35). St. John speaks of it in this way: "Dearly beloved, we are God's children now; what we shall later be has not yet come to light. We know that when it comes to light we shall be like Him, for we shall see Him as He is. Everyone who has this hope based on Him keeps himself pure, as He is pure" (*1 Jn.* 3:2-3). We are now His children. What shall we be? His bride, pure as He is pure, pure as His mother is pure.

The purity of our celibate life is pure gift. It is a gift for the kingdom that we may live like the angels, as a sign of the kingdom to come—not marrying, always present to the Lord, always ready and available to do His bidding. It is a gift. Jesus explained as He taught on the question of marriage: "Not everyone can accept this teaching, only those to whom it is given to do so...some there are who have freely renounced sex for the sake of God's reign. Let him accept this teaching who can" (*Mt.* 19:11-12).

Since it is a gift, it can be asked for in prayer, as the Second Vatican Council taught: (Referring explicitly to the Latin Church), "It (this most holy Synod) trusts in the Spirit that the gift of celibacy, which so befits the priesthood of the New Testament, will be generously bestowed by the Father, as long as those who share in Christ's priesthood through the sacrament of orders, and indeed the whole Church, humbly and earnestly pray for it" (Presbyterorum Ordinis, #16).

If we dare ask for it in prayer we will receive the gift of being a eunuch for the kingdom of God. So the question hinges around daring to ask for it. Are we really willing to live totally and completely married to the Lord? He is a jealous

God and wants no rivals or competition. Our choice must be clear and firm, not a "valeitas," a wishful thinking that some day things might be different! We must make a covenant of marriage with the Lord and then we will receive the gift of being a eunuch for the kingdom! In this case being a eunuch means that temptations of lust will not be our main problem, unless we deliberately expose ourselves to lustful situations or to pornography. And if we are suddenly attacked by lustful temptations, then as spouses of the Lord we can cry out with confident boldness, "Lord, your spouse is being molested, do you not care?!" And the Lord does answer such a plea. I know he does.

But I know from observation and from ministry that there are priests who are not married. They are in trouble, either in fact, or looking for it by being "on the make." By their manners, their dress, their style of association they are crying out by body language, "I'm available!" Others are in a "spiritual" relationship with women who supply their felt need for feminine companionship. God is a jealous God and wants us to draw all our sustenance from Him—otherwise we can enter into a "spiritual" adulterous relation, if not adulterous.

Today the Church again needs virgins and martyrs, men married to the Lord, on fire for the sake of the Kingdom, men with their bodies, minds, wills, and hearts totally given to the Lord to prepare for His coming.

A further word on dealing with lustful temptations. Distinguish the type of temptation first. If it's a strong compulsion, then take spiritual authority: "In the name of Jesus Christ and by the power of His precious Blood, I take authority over you, spirit of lust and order you to be gone, bound to Jesus. You have no place here. I am the bride of Christ."

If the temptations are pornographic imaginings, then literally pluck them out of your head and hand them over to Jesus for healing. It is good even to use a gesture of the hands and arms and observe what Jesus does with these "weeds." If the temptations have to do with a relationship with a person, then intercession is called for. "Lord, I repent of my past and I ask for mercy for that person involved. I plunge them into the infinite ocean of Your mercy."

This kind of temptation I treat as an urgent plea for

intercession—there is a person in need and I can help by my prayer, so the Lord stirs my imagination or memory in order that I pray for them. So discernment is needed, but we are given powerful weapons in deliverance, healing, and intercession.

"Everyone who has this hope based on Him keeps himself pure, as He is pure" (*1 Jn.* 3:3), pure as our Immaculate Mother.

>May our Immaculate Mother share her grace with you,
>Fr. George

30. NEED OF KNOWING JESUS CHRIST AND THE BAPTISM IN THE HOLY SPIRIT

November 22, 1985
Holy Family Hermitage

Dear Father Ed,

The Lord be with you.

I wrote to you about the *totality* of the "yes" of the commitment of Jesus and to Jesus in His three-fold baptism. In this letter I want to make the point that we cannot skip over or assume any of the steps of the three-fold baptism. I know that we cannot presume that the candidates coming to the seminary and religious life have experienced the fullness of the three-fold baptism. I would venture to say that we cannot presume this of priests, either. And what about bishops? We cannot assume that a person with a vocation *knows* (and this experientially, in the biblical sense of knowledge) the power and the presence, and the Person of the Lord Jesus Christ as He is now—not as He was historically. We need to personally lead a candidate through the various conversions needed to come to this fuller experiential knowledge. For some, this conversion may be the first conversion; for others, a second or third, and so on. No matter where we have come to in our knowledge of Jesus Christ, there is always more! "There is more. There IS more. There is so much more," Kathryn Kuhlman used to say.

Even after a person has experienced a significant conversion there is yet another step and there is more. Recall that monastic and eremitical rules call for a vow of continuous conversion. Pope John Paul II in his Holy Thursday Letter to all Priests (1979) challenged us: "We must be converted anew each day."—A continuous conversion. And that's why the baptism in the Holy Spirit is on my heart and mind at this time in the Hermitage.

A pattern of leading a person through a major conversion that I use currently is one I learned from Father Jim Ferry of Newark, N.J., who headed our team at Visitation House. It is based on the renewal of the sacraments of baptism and confirmation. It involves a time of catechesis and then a time of leading the person so that he himself prays through the basic steps of conversion that lead to a deeper surrender to the Holy Spirit and a fuller release of the Holy Spirit and his gifts. This type of instruction on prayer is right to the point and not lengthy, but it is based on a great hunger and thirst for the Lord and on an expectant faith in the Lord—that is, a faith that expects God to act because He has promised to do so.

I've used this basic pattern for hundreds and hundreds of priests—it works! And just yesterday I used it again.

For the catechesis I use the text of *John* 7:37-39 to explain the attitudes the candidate needs, then I use *Rom.* 8:26-27 and *1 Cor.* 14:1-19, to teach about prayer in tongues. Next I explain the steps of the prayer for conversion and release of the Spirit and then we pray. We conclude with a time of praise of God and a final instruction. This kind of catechesis and prayer can take place in one session if the person has been living the Christian life and knows the basics: the love of God, turning from sin and turning to the living God, and is ready to give his whole life to Him. But the more common way would be a series of a half-dozen talks and discussion in sharing prayers over a period of six or seven weeks, or on a retreat, in order to prepare for the prayer of a total "yes" to the Lord.

Let me go over this catechesis in greater detail:

Jesus cried out "If anyone thirsts, let him come to me; let him drink who believes in me. Scripture has it: 'From within him rivers of living water shall *flow*!" (*Jn.* 7:37-38, Emphasis added). Then John goes on to comment, "Here He was referring to the Spirit, whom those that came to believe in Him were to receive. There was, of course, no Spirit as yet, since Jesus had not yet been glorified" (*Jn.* 7:39)—but now Jesus had died and is risen and has sent His Holy Spirit! The five verbs in the words of Jesus—thirst, come, drink, believe and flow—describe the attitude of a person who wants to receive the Spirit. We need to thirst and to hunger and to long for the Lord more than for anything else in this world—nothing else will satisfy but the Lord alone. Are we desperate enough that we want Him alone and nobody or anything but Him?

Then we need to come to Jesus, as we are, and ask. We need to ASK for all our needs, we need to ask for everything, we need to ask for His Holy Spirit to come and possess us, and purify us, and transform us. But we also need to drink—to receive, to accept and to surrender and yield to His power, His presence and His person. We do this believing—with "expectant faith" in Jesus. He has promised to give us His Holy Spirit if we ask with faith. So we ask and expect to receive it. We wait and receive it and rejoice in it. If we come to Jesus with this kind of faith and drink—then the rivers, the Spirit, will *flow*. The Spirit will flow revealing the power, and the presence, and the Person of the Lord Jesus as He is now. We will know Him and we will know the Father and will cry out in praise. His words of Sacred Scripture will come alive in us and His words to us and through us will come as words of wisdom, discernment and prophetic utterances. His power will flow in healings, deliverances and miracles. His Spirit will flow for the building of His Church and the proclaiming of His kingdom.

And what about the gift of tongues—the prayer in tongues? It, too, is a gift of the Holy Spirit. Because we do not know how to pray as we ought, the Spirit comes to help us and himself makes intercession for us with groanings that cannot be expressed in speech. He intercedes as God Himself wills! (See *Rom.* 8:26-27). David Duplessis tells the incident at Vatican II that places the gift of tongues in its proper perspective and shows its purpose. David was invited by Pope John XXIII as an observer from the Pentecostal Churches. At one of the many small informal discussion sessions, a group of bishops asked David to tell them about the gifts of the Spirit that are part of their tradition. So David began to talk about the gift of tongues and had only made a few statements when one of the bishops interrupted asking, "Why don't you tell us about some of the gifts, the higher gifts like healing and miracles your church is supposed to have?" And David retorted, "Let me ask you some questions first!" David went on to ask, "Do you agree that the gift of tongues is a gift of the Holy Spirit and is in Sacred Scripture?" "Well, I guess we'll have to grant you that," the bishop answered hesitantly. "And do you agree further," David then went on to ask, "that the gift of tongues is the lowest of the gifts?" "Oh, yes!" the bishop quickly answered. "Then I've got you where I want you! If the gift of tongues is the lowest of the gifts," David responded, slapping the palm of his hand on the floor, "let's start at the bottom of the ladder and work our way up!" They all burst into laughter and David was free to go on about the gift of tongues.

The gift of tongues—here I am describing the prayer form and not the preaching and prophetic form—is also a gift of the Holy Spirit and should be honored as such. It is a powerful teaching tool of the Spirit to show us how to cooperate with his action in an incarnational way and so learn how to yield to the other gifts like discernment, words of knowledge, prophecy, and healings. In yielding to and in using the gift of tongues there is a cooperation on my part with the Holy Spirit—I must do my part and He must do His part. My part is to yield my vocal apparatus to Him and actually make the sound—open my mouth, move my tongue and vocal chords and make the sound *and* step out in faith—like Peter walking on the water—confident that the Spirit will do His part, that is, make these groanings into his intercession. And he is always faithful. We know by the fruit of the prayer—peace and joy and answered prayer. This kind of cooperation is a tool to teach us how to cooperate in yielding and using the other gifts. St. Paul in *1 Cor.* 14:1-19, says "I should like it if all of you spoke in tongues" (v. 5) and further, "Thank God I speak in tongues more than any of you" (v. 19). David Duplessis quoted this verse to the bishops and one of them came back with, "Yes, but the verse goes on to say, 'but in the church I would rather say five intelligible words to instruct others than ten thousand words in a tongue!'" But David wasn't without a quick refutal with his homespun exegesis of the verse. "If Paul prayed more than all of them, when did he do all this tongue work? He prayed ten thousand words in tongues *before* he said five intelligent words to the Church!" Again laughter won the day.

The prayer of tongues is an abstract prayer; it is the babbling of a child in the arms of the Father; it is a language of love and needs no translation. If we are willing to yield and surrender to the Father, even our rational speech, then he can do anything with us! We should long for, desire, ask for, yield and use the gift of tongues. It is a special prayer for intercession. It's a powerful prayer before preaching, before ministering in the sacrament of reconciliation and in the sacraments to ask for wisdom and discernment. Pray and then step out and speak.

And now on to the "prayer" for conversion and deeper surrender to the Holy Spirit. We pray in successive steps these spontaneous short prayers and have the candidate repeat them in his own words but audibly so he can hear them:

- *Lord, I repent*—of all my sins of my whole life. I am sorry for offending Your infinite mercy. Forgive me. (Sacrament of Reconciliation if appropriate).
- *Lord, I forgive*—all those who have offended me and I ask forgiveness of those whom I have offended. (Mentioning to oneself those who come to mind.)
- *I renounce you, Satan!*—and your spirit of . . . (naming any spirit that has manifested itself in compulsive action.) I take authority over you, spirit of . . . in the name of Jesus and order you to be gone, bound to Jesus.
- *Jesus, I take You as my Savior and my Lord*—Come, Lord Jesus and take over my life. I freely and willingly invite You to be Lord of my life and rule my life. (Take the time needed for personal prayer.)
- *Jesus, baptize me in Your Holy Spirit*—release within me the Holy Spirit and His gifts. Come, Holy Spirit and possess my life—purify me, fill me, transform me, sanctify me. (Take time for praise and waiting for the action of the Holy Spirit. We encourage yielding to the gift of tongues to help in prayer and to manifest a sign of his presence.) We pray with the laying on of hands.
- *Mary, Mother of God and my Mother,*—I entrust my consecrated life to you! Take me as your own and do for me what you did for Jesus.

After this we spend some time in praise of God together and rejoice and thank Him for His merciful gift of the Spirit and His gifts. At this point a warning is needed:—After Jesus was baptized in the Holy Spirit at the Jordan, the Spirit led Him into the desert to be tempted by Satan. So, we too can expect Satan to tempt us with thoughts like, "This is not for real. You're just kidding yourself." But our response must be that of the Lord—"Begone, Satan, I am a son of God; and Him alone I serve!"

Then I assign a penance because it is a renewal of the sacraments and the penance I assign is to spend some time alone with the Lord and praise and glorify Him out loud, using the gift of tongues, or yielding to it, to praise God freely for His great mercy.

So this is the pattern of leading candidates in a personal way to a deeper conversion. It is a very significant and effective conversion but there is always more. There is the more in moving on with Christ Jesus to be immersed in the bath that He was to be baptized with. God in His way and in His timing calls each of us further along the road to Jerusalem— that "Moving on!"

This kind of conversion described here, leading a candidate to come to know the Lord, or to deepen this knowledge of the Lord, cannot be passed by. It is the foundation of our spiritual life. We cannot move on unless we know the power and the presence of the person of the Lord Jesus Christ, as He is now, The Risen Lord! He is the foundation on which we build.

I've shared these reflections with you in the hope they can renew your own knowledge of the Lord and help you to lead others to the knowledge of the Lord. This type of knowledge of the Lord is essential for the spiritual life of priests, religious and laity, and all too often it has been assumed and we've ended up building the upper stones of a house without solid foundation.

Assume nothing!

In Christ Jesus our Lord,
Fr. George

31. OF SOLITUDE, TEAMS, AND FRATERNITY

> November 23, 1985
> *Holy Family Hermitage*
> *Feast of St. Columban*

Dear Father Ed,

I've been wanting to write to you about fraternity and teamwork among priests but it isn't until now that the struggle within me about the work with the Fraternity of Priests has resolved itself. By the grace of God, which has given me some new and fundamental insights into my own character make-up, I see new light and hope.

But you're the one who should be writing to me about fraternity among priests. Your small group of five priests in Detroit has been gathering weekly for almost eight years! I was with you at the beginning and a number of times since then. I know that the initial draft of your constitution, stating your goals and commitments started off with: "In order to preserve our priesthood and maintain our sanity...!" You know the value and necessity of gathering as brothers to support each other spiritually, emotionally, and even financially in these times of turmoil and travail. You've been faithful brothers to each other and this is the key element, your relationship of brotherhood shown by your faithful love and support of each other. The actual schedule of events, your sharing, your praying vespers, time of mutual ministry, preparing the coming Sunday's homily, an hour of adoration and a bag lunch are all excellent ingredients into the mix, but the real issue is your relationship as friends and brothers. You know and love one another, so then you are able to serve one another by advice, discernment and mutual presence.

The Vatican II "Decree on the Ministry and Life of Priests" gives a clear teaching and exhortation for fraternity among priests, encouraging even some form of common life or at least frequent and regular gatherings. The danger of loneliness and the value of associations to overcome it and to promote holiness and zeal among priests is recognized (see #8). Your priests' group has filled this need and more over the years.

These past two years I've been part of the Visitation House Team of four priests at the University of Steubenville, promoting local fraternity groups among priests. We used as a working model the priests' fraternity in Providence, Rhode Island, that meets weekly for three events: praise of God, a teaching, and ministry in small groups. There is a leader and assistant leader of the eighteen priests who have the responsibility of pastorally serving the priests. As a team of four, a two by two, we've traveled across and around the United States, into Canada, and were twice to Ireland, England, and Scotland, promoting these groups and conducting workshops on how to set up a local fraternity. The results? Some two dozen groups, varying in size from two to twenty are under way. The results are minimal but significant.

In August, in Wareham, Massachusetts, we held a leader's week of brotherhood and sharing, trying to foster a relationship between the fifteen leaders that could attend. It was a very blessed week but we realized a number of tensions arising in this work. Father Carl Hammer, of Albuquerque, New Mexico, asked, "What do you do with the men who have publicly committed themselves to come together weekly but don't come regularly? We always have a handful but never the same ones!"

Father John Dreher of our team said, "Point out to them the effect that non-attendance has on a group. It says, 'I have something more important than you.' It is very destructive of any group."

Father Bob Bedard of Ottawa, Ontario, said, "They aren't desperate enough!"

There was a different tension at the other end of the spectrum. Father Ken Gallagher of Langton, North Dakota, has a very strong and faithful fraternity. Because of the tremendous distances they must travel, they are meeting overnight every other week to give more time to each other. In fact, they are now thinking of meeting overnight every week! And they want to move into team ministry. Father John Dreher's reaction to this was: "This is good for you and you should experiment; but the Visitation House Team can't help you, and the other fraternities aren't that far along. It is best to go slowly on that until your relationships are strong."

In all of this, where have I been personally? I've had a hard time being part of the team but I've enjoyed being part of the fraternity with priests. The insight into *why* is an important one for me and it is very obvious once I've looked at it from the point of view of my whole priestly ministry. I related to Father Charles my journey from biochemistry, to giving retreats to priests, to the house of intercession, and now to Visitation House. The insight came from Father Charles' response. He said simply, "You're not a team man! Your Polish temperament needs freedom to preach and do things and not be held down by a team." Like a flash, I saw the various experiences of my life in this light and how true and perceptive his response was. In my biochemistry days I was a one-man team: teaching, researching and writing; and then from 1970 to 1975, I was a one-man Retreat Team, supported in prayer by the community in Ann Arbor and later in Detroit. It was a time of being very free in preaching and writing. Then, with Bethany House of Intercession from 1975 to 1983, I was free at first but gradually began to feel caged in, especially in giving team retreats to priests. It seemed that more of my energy went toward ministry and concern for the team than to retreatants. These past two years with the Visitation House Team I've been even more caged, less free, working with a team. My greater concern was to please the team rather than please God and serve the men with freedom.

Yet, not being able to enter into teamwork has not been incompatible with living a community life. Father Jim Ferry, our founding leader of Visitation House has a tremendous gift for initializing programs, seeing talents and characteristics immediately and making use of them. On his departure back to his parish last year and several times since, he has said to me, "You're the easiest man to live with that I have ever met." This, too, can come from my ability to please people and from my need for their affirmation.

Father Charles went on to point out that I may not be a team man, but I am a peace-maker. I can do things quickly and efficiently if I don't have to depend on others who usually prevent me from accomplishing the task with dispatch because of their different sense of timing or different capabilities.

These characteristics pointed out by Father Charles have also given me an insight into my TV work. Over the past two years I did some forty TV shows, thirteen of them as a host and the rest as a teacher. I found that I was free! In fact, the thirteen shows for Mother Angelica on The Divine Mercy devotion, and the seventeen shows for Father John Bertolucci on our Lady were like an oasis of joy during some very dark times. I guess I have a "teacher's complex," that is, "name the topic and face me toward the audience!"

These insights into my character are helping me to understand why I've been like oil on water in regard to the Visitation House Team and now, here at Holy Family Hermitage, I'm experiencing a new freedom, a new joy, and a new productivity! I can't remember so prolonged and continuous a time of presence of the Lord in my heart and joy on my face. I need solitude within community. I need freedom in apostolic work.

Another insight and dimension as to fraternity and teams started with the homily this morning. I started with the gospel of the day, *Luke* 20:27-40, on the seven brothers and the one wife on the day of resurrection, and pointed out that we are able to be like the angels who stand in the presence of the Lord and see His face, always ready and available to do His bidding. The angels have a threefold characteristic that reflects the nature of Jesus, Who is *disciple* of the Father, totally submissive to Him and hears Him and acts on the Father's word; and Who is *apostle* of the Father, sent by Him with full authority to carry out His plan; and Who is a *companion* and co-equal to the Father as True God and Son in the unity of the Holy Spirit. So the angels are *disciples,* totally present and available; they are *apostles,* sent with authority as messengers of salvation; and they are *companions* to the Lord, ministering to Him and have the company of one another in singing God's praises.

To my delight this triplet recalled an old favorite teaching on being disciples, apostles, and companions of the Lord as recorded for us in *Mark* 1:16-20 (published in *The Key to the Good News:* Jesus Christ is Lord, Dove Publications, Pecos, NM 87552, 1975). It is the scene where Jesus calls His first four disciples. Peter and Andrew were frustrated after a night of fishing but catching nothing. Jesus called them to follow as His disciples and then they would be fishers of men—real apostles. Then He called James and John, who were in the company of their father and the hired men, mending their nets (a word used by the early church to mend community relations). They left that company and went off in the company of the Lord. The three elements are here with a very definite priority on discipleship. Follow the Lord first and foremost, then you can be sent as an apostle, and be in His company as brother. The priority is on being His disciple and then His apostle and His companion.

Here at Holy Family Hermitage I see this triple element expressed in solitude as the priority of discipleship. By solitude and in solitude all is given to God alone. This is Blessed Paul Giustiniani's maxim—"All for God alone!" God first and foremost. This solitude is supported by a community of brothers who serve one another in the needs of daily life, who express their common apostolate of prayer and intercession in their common celebration of the Eucharistic Liturgy, and in the chanting of the Liturgy of the Hours.

And in my own life, because of my experience of solitude in the hermitage, and because of the current insight into my character of being a community man but not a team man, I can see that my future apostolic work will need to be carried on out of a community and also out of solitude, but not as a member of a team. This can mean working with a companion or a servant of the Lord where I can be free to express the insights and teachings the Lord has given me by His grace.

How this will express itself in the future I don't know. What I do know, however, is the word that has been on my heart and has been repeated several times: "Be faithful to Me; I am preparing something for you that you do not expect." Working in this freer way, out of a community and out of solitude is certainly something I wouldn't have expected three months ago! This pattern of being sent as an apostle out of support of both community and solitude is the pattern proposed by many religious communities. It certainly has a great and growing attraction for me. I'm trying to be faithful to the Lord and waiting to see what He has prepared.

> In Jesus, the Disciple and Apostle of the Father, and our elder Brother,
> Fr. George

32. THE HEART OF THE PRIEST

November 25, 1985
Holy Family Hermitage

Dear Father Ed,

I have a real challenge before me. I want to write about the heart of the priest, the heart in the biblical sense of man's human spirit that longs for God. So, how can I write rationally about the heart? My biochemical background comes to the fore and I want to analyze and define and distinguish. And yet, during this time of solitude, the desires of the heart, the prayer of the heart have been so important. So, the way that I'll approach this letter, then, is to make some distinctions and definitions to remove some obstacles and thus set the stage for some very personal reflections of my heart on priesthood. I hope that they won't be too personal, but I'll share them as they are.

The human heart is the term used in sacred scripture for the human spirit. It is this spirit that communes with God; it is the touch-point of the Holy Spirit and is the seat of His love and presence. The Holy Spirit is poured into our hearts (*Rom.* 5:5) and it is the Holy Spirit that the Church asks to fill out hearts.

It is fascinating to me that the Church prays "fill the hearts of the faithful" (oration of Pentecost) and does not say fill the heads of the faithful! The human spirit, the heart, is supposed to be queen of our faculties, not our own rationality as we have made it. The Holy Spirit enters our persons by way of our human spirit, as through a gate, and His presence sets our hearts on fire. He enkindles them with the fire of divine love. It is this fire of the Holy Spirit that in turn illumines our minds. The presence of the Holy Spirit is a Tabor experience that makes us radiate with His grace. This is the spirituality of the Eastern Fathers; it is a transfiguration, a divinization. His presence makes the "morning star" (*Rev.* 2:28; *Phil.* 2:15) rise in our hearts (*2 Ptr.* 1:19). He transforms our hearts.

The heart of the priest is to be the heart of Jesus who said of Himself: "Come to Me. . . for I am gentle and humble of heart" (*Mt.* 11:28-30). To be priests after the heart of Jesus we need a heart transplant! We need the heart of Jesus Himself so that we can love with His Heart; so that we can serve with His Heart, so that we can preach with His Heart, so that we can pray with His Heart; so that in His Heart we can listen in the "Heart" of the Father.

Love with the Heart of Jesus

Over the years I've wanted to love the Lord but never seemed to know how to do it or just what to do. But there were specific times when I expressed my desire to love the Lord. At home, when I was talking with Mother while she was hanging up the laundry in the basement, I said, "If we're supposed to love God with our whole heart, I guess the best thing I could do is to be a priest." This was the first time I expressed my vocation, and that in chop logic. During high school days I fell in love with a girl but told her that my love for God came first and she respected that. At the time of my first vows on August 15, 1947, the Feast of the Assumption of Our Lady, I wept with joy in giving myself to the Lord. Through the years of the seminary, I tried to love God. The one special moment that stands out was in fourth year theology, while reading Louis Bouyer's *Liturgical Piety*. My heart was set on fire for the Lord by the section on "The mystery, Christ in you, the hope of glory" (*Col.* 1:27). I recall how I went to lunch with one hundred seminarians and was aware of how much the Lord loved each one of us. What stands out in my memory of my ordination day is the time after the laying on of hands and the anointing of my hands when I was rubbing in the sacred oil and reflecting, "I am a priest."

Over the years I've been a "yo-yo," sometimes up, sometimes down; but more and more I've come to the realization that I was the Lord's yo-yo, and He is faithful and loves me whether I'm up or down.

Another way that I've experienced His love has been both by His presence and by His absence. When He was present, I would be occupied with Him; and when absent, I would be preoccupied wondering where He was. Whether present or absent it seems to have been a journey of seeking Him. Despite my falls, He has been faithful in His mercy, seeking me!

During these months in solitude, the presence of the Lord has been the dominant grace. More and more my heart is going out to Him and I want to love Him with my whole heart. I realized that the first description of how we are to love God is with our "whole heart" (*Deut.* 6:5 and *Matt.* 22:37). As I came into the hermitage, the song that was on my heart expressed this: "Change my heart, O God, make it ever true. Change my heart, Oh God, may I be like You" (Eddie Espinosa).

One early morning last week my prayer was a desire of the heart for the Lord, in the arms of Mary. I wrote a prayer afterwards. "Fill me, Lord, with Your Holy Spirit. I want to do Your will. I don't want to waste any of Your graces of this solitude. Cleanse me, heal me, transfigure me into Your image, to radiate Your mercy."

Later that day I read in *Our Lady Speaks to Her Beloved Priests:*

> "I will give to your heart my own capacity to love...to bring you to a simple, continuous and pure act of love. My joy is to bring you to love, so that my own Heart may love, within yours, the most Holy and Divine Trinity" (January 13, 1977).

Celebration of Mass (Feast of Dedication of the Basilicas of Saints Peter and Paul) followed and I preached from the texts: "Proclaim the Kingdom of Jesus and keep your eyes fixed on Jesus" and ended up with "Let your hearts love Him." At communion time, a word flowed from within my heart that I wrote down afterwards:

> I give you My own heart in exchange for yours, so that you may love Me and the Father with My Heart, so that you may love Mary, My Mother and yours, with My Heart. This is a very special gift, George. Accept it, use it and rejoice in it. Always love Me with your whole Heart. Love the Father with My Heart, into which He had poured the Holy

Spirit. Love Mary with My Heart. George, rejoice! Rejoice! Rejoice! I have given you a great treasure, not for any worth or merit of yours, but a sheer gift. Praise Me. Rejoice and love Me!

My response? "Thank You, thank You, thank You! I love You with the Heart of Mary. May she love You in my Heart, now Yours. Jesus, I love You, save souls. Father, I love You with the Heart of Jesus, filled with the Spirit. I love you, Mary, with the Heart of your Son Jesus."

All this came with a great anointing, a quickening of the heart and a flow of energy, like waves, the tensor muscles flexing. My head doesn't grasp this, but my heart has been moved and it leaps—

"Lord, I accept Your Heart. I want to be faithful to You— help me. I do want to love You with my whole heart. Please do not let me get in the way with sin, or with my head, or with my 'antsiness,' or whatever. I really want to love You with my whole heart. I want Mary to teach me to love God and my neighbor ever more and more."

I sense that I need to let my heart go—and love. No words, no analyzing, but an attentive presence of love and the embrace of my heart.

November 26, 1985

All this happened after a very special night of sleep. Nine hours—with only one break. I haven't slept like that for years!

On further reflection on this gift of the Lord's Heart I realized that this is the grace of this time of solitude: His love for me and His Heart to love in return. Probably the best thanksgiving for this gift is to use it—to love Him with my whole heart.

I took some more time in thanksgiving before the Blessed Sacrament, pondering this word, rereading the section in *Our Lady Speaks to Her Beloved Priests* (January 13, 1977) and then a word from Mary stirred in my heart:

> George, I love you very, very much. I give you my own Heart so that you may love Jesus with my Heart. And so love the Father with both our Hearts beating together. In this way my Heart will be honored along with that of my Son as He so desires! Accept and use this precious gift of my Heart.

"Mary, I accept it in my weakness and I will use it—to honor Jesus, to love Him as you love Him—to love and honor the Father with your Heart in union with His! Thank you, thank you, thank you, Mother. I so need to be filled with love. I'm so empty without you. Teach me how to love God and to love my neighbor more and more.

"Such joy, such peace, such love can only come from you. Thank You, Jesus. Thank you, Mary. Thank You, Holy Spirit of Jesus and spouse of Mary. Come, Holy Spirit, fill my heart more and more to honor, love, and adore the Sacred and Blessed Trinity in the Heart of Mary.

"I don't need to say anything but I do need to let my heart flow and radiate with love for You."

The heart of the priest is to be the Heart of Jesus, to love the Father, and to love His people with the Heart of Jesus.

Serve with the Heart of Jesus

I wish I really could serve with the Heart of Jesus. This is what the Church in effect tells us to do when through the ordaining bishop we are asked: "Are you resolved to celebrate the mysteries of Christ (the Sacraments) faithfully and religiously as the Church has handed them down to us for the glory of God and the sanctification of Christ's people?" (Second question of the Ordination Rite, Roman Liturgy).

In prayer today I realized that serving with the Heart of Christ means serving with a pierced heart—with Blood and Water flowing, signs of His mercy given in Baptism, Reconciliation, and Eucharist. It means that I must unite my broken heart with His pierced Heart and be as compassionate as He is, in ministering the sacraments. In the sacramental ministry I'm not just a functionary but I am a living channel of God's mercy.

The Second Vatican Council's "Decree on Ministry and Life of the Priest" speaks of our serving with "Pastoral love" (#14) which means to serve with the Heart of the Shepherd, with the Heart of Jesus. And He laid down His life for His sheep.

I've a long way to go to serve with the Heart of Jesus. I can't do it—so Lord, I ask for Your Heart to serve Your Church.

Preach with the Heart of Jesus

Jesus preached with His Heart pouring out His mercy so that the crowds were both spellbound by His words, and also touched by His mercy in healing, delivering, and feeding. He preached with such power of the Spirit, that hearts were opened and transformed.

Would that I could preach with the Heart of Jesus and have the hearers moved to know, to love, and to serve the Lord. This too the Church has ordained me to do as said through the lips of the ordaining bishop: "Are you resolved to exercise the ministry of the word worthily, preaching the Gospel and explaining the Catholic faith?" (Third question of the Ordination Rite.)

These three months at the Hermitage I've had the extraordinary privilege of preaching daily at the Liturgy of the Eucharist. I've never had the opportunity to preach daily for such an extended period of time. I try to approach each day's readings in prayer the day before, asking the Lord, "Lord, what do You want said to us in this Liturgy?" I read over the texts, jot down key phrases that strike me; and then ask the Lord to teach me. Sometimes a word to proclaim comes immediately, but most of the time it is a moment of trust as I set the text aside and go on with my other duties. The next morning in prayer I am usually flooded with insights on the liturgy of the day—to say this, to look up that, and so on. I pray for my brothers that they may hear what they need to hear. At the prayer before the gospel, I pray that I may be purified to proclaim His word. I ask that the anointing of God come down upon me and my brothers and that the Lord be glorified and we be built up in faith. Then away I go. Afterwards, especially in thanksgiving after Communion, I rejoice in what the Lord did in the proclamation of the word and usually a particular phrase or word remains to feed me. During these months of daily preaching I've been consciously ending the homily with a tie into the celebration of this particular Eucharist. I've led the Prayers of the Faithful, using the theme of the word just proclaimed.

To preach with the Heart of Jesus means that I must have His Heart and His Mind. Since this is a gift of the Spirit, I need to ask for it: "Lord, I ask for Your Heart to preach to Your people."

Pray with the Heart of Jesus

To pray with the Heart of Jesus means to pray as He prayed—and He prayed, "Abba." He taught us to pray "Abba" and to hallow His name, to ask that His kingdom come, that His will be done. When Jesus taught His disciples how to pray He really taught them how He lived—all for the Father!

The prayer of Jesus was more than words; He prayed with His whole Heart, His whole being, in union with the Father. He prayed with His Heart full of love and honor for the Father, full of thanksgiving. Jesus prayed out of the awareness of the presence of the love of the Father. He radically trusted the Father with His whole Heart. He knew the Father's love for Him.

It seems to me that to pray is, first of all, to be present in love, to be present with our heart, and from that presence the prayers will flow. So there is something prior and more important than saying prayers, and that is to be present to the Father. In order to do this we need the Heart of Jesus Himself. And we ask for it—"Jesus, I need Your Heart to pray like You. Please give me Your Heart."

During this time of solitude, prayer of the heart has been growing in prominence—just being present to the Lord with my heart, letting it flow with love for Him—no words, just a flow of love. From the anointing of His presence I try to express my prayer of intercession, my priestly prayer in various ways: foremost, the prayer of the Eucharist and the Liturgy of the Hours. I also offer the Chaplet of The Divine Mercy once or twice a day, making a continuous novena for the needs of the Church. I pray the full rosary for various intentions, but I'm not very good at praying the rosary—I keep getting distracted, but I keep at it. Generally, I find I'm like a butterfly with my mind flitting from one flower to another. I hope the Lord likes butterflies—at least He wants me to be a monarch, as long as I stay in His garden. So, to overcome this butterfly flitting of my mind, I've tried to practice, as a priority, the presence of my heart to the Lord and pray often, "Come, Holy Spirit, and fill my heart. Come, Spirit of the Father and the Son. Come, Spouse of Mary, purify me, possess me, love and transform me, do whatever needs to be done. Do it."

Mary, in *Our Lady Speaks to Her Beloved Priests* (July 29, 1977), speaks of her Immaculate Heart as a garden wherein the Father delights as in His plan perfectly realized; where the Son finds His habitual dwelling place; and where the Spirit is the gardener, the source of water and its light. Mary has given this gardener of her Heart to priests who have consecrated themselves to her. I guess that's where this butterfly belongs!

November 27, 1985

Listen with the Heart of Jesus

Jesus said that what He heard from the Father He tells us:

> ...I only tell the world what I have heard from Him, the truthful One Who sent Me...I say only what the Father has taught Me... (*Jn.* 8:26-29).

Jesus listened and did the will of the Father. The blessing He directed to Mary and to those who listen applies to Himself in a perfect way: "Blest are they who hear the word of God and keep it" (*Lk.* 11:28).

Jesus in giving the greatest command quotes from *Deuteronomy* 6:4, beginning with "Hear, O Israel! The Lord our God is Lord alone!" Then He follows with "Therefore you shall love the Lord your God with all your heart..." (*Mk.* 12:29-30). We must listen and hear the Lord to love Him.

Our western civilization has a problem with listening because it thinks that the ear is attached to the head—we listen with our minds, analyzing, comparing, distinguishing. But the Hebraic sense of the ear is that it is attached to the heart! How do like that anatomy! Yes, the ear is attached to the heart and it is in this way we listen and hear the word of God. When King Solomon asked for an "understanding heart to judge your people and to distinguish right from wrong" (*1 Kgs.* 3:9), he asked for a "heart with an ear on it."

We as priests need this kind of heart. We need circumcised hearts; hearts open to the word of God; hearts that are pure and attached only to the Lord. Nothing hardens the heart to the whispering of the Lord's word more than attachments of the heart to things other than the Lord. Would that I could be single-hearted, totally given and present to the Lord.

This is the grace of this sabbatical of solitude. I set, as my first priority, listening to the Lord. Then I asked Him to teach me how to listen and what it means to listen. The one word that came immediately was "presence." To listen is to be present to Him. Now I would add, to listen to the Lord is to be present with my heart in His Heart. To listen is to abide in His love (*Jn.* 15:1-17).

The heart of the Priest must be the Heart of Jesus! To be Jesus in the world, we need to have His Heart to love, to serve, to preach, to pray, and to listen. And Mary has been given to us as a mother who takes us into her Heart and places us in the burning furnace of the Heart of her son—the Heart of Mercy.

In the Heart of Jesus,
Fr. George

33. DEVOTION TO THE DIVINE MERCY

November 27, 1985
Holy Family Hermitage

Dear Father Ed,

As you've read through these letters you are by now aware of the centrality of The Divine Mercy in my life, and perhaps see how it ought to be central to our priesthood.

In this letter I want to reflect on the devotion to The Divine Mercy as revealed to Sister M. Faustina Kowalska (1905-1938) of Cracow, Poland. You can get an excellent pamphlet on the *Devotion to The Divine Mercy* from the Marian Helpers Center, Stockbridge, MA 01263 (#M-17), compiled by Father Seraphim Michalenko, M.I.C. You'll recall that he was a team member at Bethany House of Intercession at the time when on April 15, 1978, the rescript of the Holy See lifted the ban on the devotion. He taught us a great deal about the devotion and while with us got a fundamental insight into the priestly nature of the devotion. He was so knowledgeable on the devotion, that his community, who were originally and principally responsible for promulgating the devotion outside of Poland, called Seraphim back to reopen the department. They had closed down the department on The Divine Mercy when the prohibition of this devotion came from the Holy See on March 7, 1959.

The prohibition was caused mainly by a poor French translation of the Polish Diary of Sister Faustina which was translated into the Italian and read by the Vatican Congregation. The words of Sister Faustina, and those of the Lord to her, were not clearly indicated and thus confused. A Polish bishop who did not give up was Bishop Karol Wojtyla, who initiated the process toward her canonization. The Reverand

Professor Ignacy Rozycki, a renown Polish theologian was asked to study the matter for the process of beatification. Twenty years later, all was cleared up with a virtual apology from the Holy See (Supreme Congregation of the Holy Office in 1959, and now called the Congregation for the Doctrine of the Faith). Six months to the day after the rescript was published, the initiator of the cause of Sister Faustina was elected Bishop of Rome, John Paul II! This devotion has had a significant influence on the encyclical "Rich in Mercy" (Dives in Misericordia"), which can be fully understood only when read out of the context of the revelations given to Sister Faustina (from Archbishop Deskur's commentary on "Dives in Misericordia"). A few more fascinating tidbits. When, in 1981, the Marians of Stockbridge printed the definitive edition of the *Diary of Sr. Faustina* in its original Polish, they delivered a copy to Archbishop Andrzej Deskur, who in turn mentioned it to the Holy Father. John Paul II immediately asked, "Where is my copy?" The next day they delivered a paperback copy to him, and later a white leather-bound copy. Then, during the time of his recuperation after the attempted assassination, he had someone read it to him!

And so, what is this devotion? It is not "just another devotion." Rather, it is what a devotion ought to be, in the root sense of the word—a consecration, a dedication by solemn vow. In this sense the "devotion" to The Divine Mercy is a total commitment to His mercy—to be merciful as He is merciful.

The devotion was brought into new prominence by the revelations of Our Lord to Sister Faustina, which began in 1924 and continued until her death in 1938. The message of the Lord is one of "mercy." The Lord asks especially for trust in His mercy, that we implore His mercy (in particular for sinners and the dying), that we honor His mercy by accepting it, that we proclaim His mercy, and that we be merciful to one another. This is the heart of the Gospel!

Of course, the Sacraments of The Holy Eucharist and of Reconciliation are unique and pre-eminent channels of God's Mercy, as are the other sacrament as well. But in addition to these, the Lord has given us other means of drawing down His mercy upon ourselves. Among these is devotion to His mercy in the form given us through Sister Faustina. Its principal elements are: an image of The Divine Mercy with the inscription "Jesus, I Trust in You"; a chaplet of The Divine Mercy; a Feast of The Divine Mercy; and the request of Our Lord to remember His passion and pray at the hour of His dying on the cross. A further description of these elements of the devotion will show how it is a priestly devotion.

The Image of The Divine Mercy

Our Lord asked that Sister Faustina have an image painted after the pattern she saw, and that this would be a vessel to draw mercy from the infinite ocean of mercy. The image is of Jesus coming toward us with His right hand raised in blessing and His left hand touching His garment at the breast in the area of the heart where two rays of light shine forth, one red and the other pale. He is dressed in a white garment and is radiant with light. This image is an icon which presents three scriptural scenes, like a triple-exposure photograph. The obvious scene is Easter Sunday night when Jesus appeared coming through the locked doors of the Cenacle, with the victorious blessing of peace, showing His wounds, giving His apostles the authority He had just received and breathing on them the Holy Spirit for the forgiveness of sins (*Jn.* 20:19-31). The second scene is that of Calvary where His side was pierced and blood and water flowed out, here seen as the red and pale rays representing the cleansing water of Baptism and the life-giving Blood of the Eucharist. The third scene is that of Jesus as the eternal High Priest, dressed in the white linen of the priest coming out from the Holy of Holies—this time not from the sanctuary made by human hands, but from the mercy seat in Heaven itself—coming as the "Merciful One" with blessing in His raised hand and the name of the Lord on His lips (*Sirach* 50:18-21 and *Leviticus* 16:1-4).

A copy of this image has been hanging in my room since 1946. When I left for the novitiate of the Basilian Fathers, my mother gave it to me. It has been a continuous reminder of His mercy. The subscription in Polish: "Jezu Ufam Tobie!" (Jesus, I Trust in You!) says it all. Jesus, You are Mercy Itself and I a sinner come in confidence to the infinite ocean of Your mercy.

The Feast of The Divine Mercy

Our Lord asked Sister Faustina to pray and to initiate a feast of The Divine Mercy, on the Sunday after Easter. This would be a day of total forgiveness of sins for those who approach the Eucharist and the Sacrament of Reconciliation. It would be an annual celebration of the Day of Atonement. All would be washed clean in His infinite mercy. The texts of the Liturgy for that Sunday are already on forgiveness (The scene of Jesus appearing in the Cenacle, *Jn.* 20), and on mercy (*Ps.* 118; *1 Ptr.* 1:3-9).

For five years I have been celebrating the day as the Feast of The Divine Mercy. Incidentally, the Archdiocese of Cracow has permission for a new Votive Mass of The Divine Mercy. These celebrations have been grand continuations of the Easter celebration.

The Novena

In preparation for the Feast of Mercy, the Lord asked for a novena of prayer beginning on Good Friday and ending on the Saturday after Easter. The matter for each day's prayer was given to Sister Faustina by the Lord and it reflects the Good Friday intercessions of the liturgy—prayer for all of mankind, especially sinners, for priests, and religious brothers and sisters, for the devout, for those who don't know the Lord, for the separated brethren, for the meek and humble, for those who glorify His mercy, for the souls in Purgatory, and for the lukewarm.

The past two years I've had the opportunity to preach the novena at the Shrine of The Divine Mercy in Stockbridge, Massachusetts, and then last year as a TV novena for Mother Angelica on EWTN. These novenas were one of the highlights of each year. As I have already mentioned, during this time of solitude I've prayed a continuous novena for the needs of the Church.

The Chaplet of The Divine Mercy

The Chaplet of The Divine Mercy is an intercessory prayer that extends the offering of the Eucharist. It is a priestly prayer, prayed on the rosary beads. It begins with the Our Father, Hail Mary, and The Creed. Then, on the large beads, the following prayer is said: "Eternal Father, I offer You the Body and Blood, Soul and Divinity of Your dearly beloved Son, Our Lord Jesus Christ, in atonement for our sins and those of the whole world." On the ten small beads: "For the sake of His sorrowful Passion, have mercy on us and on the whole world." In conclusion, the following is prayed three times: "Holy God, Holy Mighty One, Holy Immortal One, have mercy on us and on the whole world."

This chaplet is part of my daily intercessory prayer. I've learned to chant it both in English and in Polish. There seems to be a special anointing in chanting it in the original language!

The Three O'Clock Prayer

The Lord asked Sister Faustina to pray especially for sinners at three o'clock in the afternoon, the moment of His death on the cross. He said that this is the hour of great mercy for the world. It is a great time to stop and pray—much better than a coffee break! It is a prayer break for a moment of reflection on His passion and death for us. It is a good time to make a visit to the Blessed Sacrament, if possible, and an excellent time for making the Stations of the Cross.

Words of Our Lord to Priests about Mercy

In her diary, Sister Faustina recorded various words of our Lord concerning the devotion to The Divine Mercy that are directed specifically to us priests. I'll quote some of the pertinent passages from the 82 revelations about the devotion as indicated by Father Ignancy Rozycki:

- I desire that **priests** preach this great mercy of Mine toward souls of sinners. Let the sinner not be afraid to approach Me. The flames of Mercy are burning Me, clamoring to be spent; I want to pour them out upon these souls (Diary, 50).

And again the Lord said to her with kindness:

- My daughter, speak to priests about this inconceivable mercy of Mine. The flames of mercy are burning Me, clamoring to be spent; I want to keep pouring them out upon souls. Souls just do not want to believe in My goodness (D. 177).

    No soul will be justified until it turns with confidence to My mercy, and this is why the first Sunday after Easter is to be the Feast of Mercy. On that day, **priests** are to tell everyone about My great and unfathomable mercy (D. 570).

Tell My priests that hardened sinners will repent on hearing their words, when they will speak about My unfathomable mercy, about the compassion I have for them in My Heart. To **priests** who will proclaim and extol My mercy, I will give wonderful power, and I will anoint their words and touch the hearts of those to whom they will speak (D. 1521).

Say unceasingly the chaplet that I have taught you. Whoever will recite it will receive great mercy at the hour of death. **Priests** will recommend it to sinners as their last hope of salvation. Even if there were a sinner most hardened, if he recites this chaplet only once, he will receive grace from My infinite mercy. I desire that the whole world know My infinite mercy. I desire to grant unimaginable graces to those souls who trust in My mercy (D. 687).

Write, speak of My mercy. Tell souls where they are to look for solace; that is, at the Tribunal of Mercy [the Sacrament of Reconciliation.] There the greatest miracles take place [and] are incessantly repeated. To avail oneself of this miracle, it is not necessary to go on a great pilgrimage or to carry out some external ceremony; it suffices to come with faith to the feet of **My representative** and to reveal to him one's misery, and the miracle of Divine Mercy will be fully demonstrated. Were a soul like a decaying corpse so that from a human standpoint there would be no [hope of] restoration and everything would already be lost, it is not so with God. The miracle of Divine Mercy restores that soul in full. Oh, how miserable are those who do not take advantage of this miracle of God's mercy! You will call out in vain, but it will be too late! (D. 1448).

What words of strength and consolation! Jesus wants His mercy made known and wants His priests to proclaim it and especially to tell sinners about it. The promise of anointing the priest's words and the hearts of his listeners when he proclaims and glorifies the Lord's mercy is an exciting promise and challenges me to take advantage of it. I've consciously and regularly spoken of the Lord's infinite ocean of mercy and I have seen the effect it has on listeners.

On the other hand, however, the Lord is deeply saddened by chosen souls—especially priests and religious—who do not turn to His mercy and do not understand it:

> My heart is sorrowful because even chosen souls do not understand the greatness of My mercy. Their relationship [with Me] is, in certain ways, imbued with mistrust. Oh, how much that wounds My Heart! Remember My Passion, and if you do not believe My words, at least believe My wounds (D. 379).

The devotion to The Divine Mercy, in a sense, is capsulized in the beatitude: "Blessed are the merciful for they shall obtain mercy." Those who are merciful to others—by thought, word and deed—will themselves obtain mercy because only the merciful can obtain mercy. Jesus Himself is the first and foremost Man of mercy and He obtained mercy from the Father and was raised from the dead to new life and ascended to the throne of the Father. Jesus trusted in the merciful Father and has commanded us to "Be merciful, even as your Father is merciful" (*Lk.* 6:36, RSV).

Again, as I said earlier, the short prayer, "Jesus, I trust in You!" is also a capsulization of the devotion to The Divine Mercy. Jesus wants to have mercy on all. To trust Him we must be merciful; to be merciful we must trust Him. He alone is the source of mercy. In Him alone we place our trust.

One of the major graces of this time of solitude has been the growing urgency to proclaim the Lord's mercy. I now see that it needs to become the major thrust of my apostolate. The times are so urgent because the Lord's Day of Judgment is approaching. There are so many souls that are in sin and darkness and do not even know about this mercy of God. Now is the time to proclaim His mercy—this is the day of mercy prior to His coming in judgment.

This is how our Lord spoke to Sister Faustina about the day of mercy and the day of justice. While she was saying the chaplet one day, she heard:

> Write down these words, My daughter. Speak to the world about My mercy; let all mankind recognize My unfathomable mercy. It is a sign for the end times; after it will come the day of justice. While there is still time, let them have recourse to the fount of My mercy; let them profit from the Blood and Water which gushed forth for them (D. 848)...Secretary of My mercy, write, tell souls about this great mercy of Mine, because the awful day, the day of My justice, is near (D. 965).

And a final example of His many revelations on the day of mercy. When Sister Faustina asked Jesus how He could tolerate so many sins and crimes and not punish them, the Lord answered her:

> I have eternity for punishing [these], and so I am prolonging the time of mercy for the sake of [sinners]. But woe be to them if they do not recognize this time of My visitation. My daughter, secretary of My mercy, your duty is not only to write about and proclaim My mercy, but also to beg for this grace for them, so that they too may glorify My mercy (D. 1160).

How much more is it the duty of each of us priests to proclaim and beg for mercy for the people—while there is still time on this day of mercy. This is the urgency that is grasping me during this time of solitude. This is devotion to The Divine Mercy.

In the mercy of Our Lord Jesus Christ,
Fr. George

34. THE PRIEST AS MYSTERY OF MERCY AND MARY

November 30, 1985
Holy Family Hermitage

Dear Father Ed,

As I come to the end of this series of reflections on the priesthood, the thought that is uppermost in my heart and mind is that the priest is mystery—a mystery of the Lord's mercy and he is the mystery of Mary.

As you recall, the sense of priest as mystery was awakened in me at the World-wide Retreat for Priests and Deacons in Rome, October 1984. Father Raniero Cantalamessa described the priesthood as a "ministry and a mystery." Since then, I've reflected on those words, commented on them and, in fact, developed them into a major teaching. Now, after having written these letters, I want to reflect on the mystery of the priesthood in light of this time of solitude.

Mystery of Mercy

The priest shares in the Mystery of Christ's condescension and His ascension which are a twofold flow of one act of love. Out of His love for sinful man He emptied Himself for our salvation. And out of that same oblation of love He glorified the Father. Christ our eternal High Priest, the mystery of mercy, has ordained us to share in this mystery. In the one priest, Jesus Christ, we both glorify the Father and glorify mankind by bringing them salvation in the Church. So we are called to a union with Him and a "sacramental identification" with Him (John Paul II, *Dominicae Cenae*, #8). Now that is a mystery! And further, as Christ perpetuated this mystery, out of His merciful love in the Eucharist, we too perpetuate our love in living the Eucharist.

The issue dealt with in this twofold flow of merciful love is SIN. Mercy is, above all, God's covenant love poured out for the forgiveness of our sins and secondly, mercy is the sacrificial love glorifying the Father in reparation for our sins. From this same merciful love flow the two basic sacraments of priesthood, namely, the Eucharist and Reconciliation (seen as the application and extension of Baptism). So, the purpose of priesthood is to glorify God and to glorify man in God!

This mystery of mercy can be described in yet another way. By our priesthood we participate in Christ's redemptive incarnation. As Christ's incarnation was a marriage with mankind and His redemption an offering of the body given Him (*Heb.* 10:5-14), we too enter into a marriage and into an offering of our bodies (*Rom.* 12:1). St. Paul compares Christ's love for the Church to marriage: "Husbands, love your wives, as Christ loved the church and gave Himself up for her. . ." (*Eph.* 5:32).

This now brings me to the other dimension of the mystery of our priesthood—the mystery of Mary and the Church.

Mystery of Mary—Church

Our priesthood shares in some of the mystery of Mary as Mother of Christ and Mother of the Church. Like her, we too have dimensions of our priesthood that are virginal, spousal, and maternal. Like Mary, we too are to be virginal—open only to the will of God and His plan. We are to be espoused—in a marriage union with the Lord by the Holy Spirit. We too are to be maternal—fruitful in bringing forth the life of Christ. As priests we are married to the Church.

Like Mary, we participate in the mystery of mercy and in the mystery of the Church. And all of this is gift. We do not create church, rather we receive it. And so, my wrap-up conclusion:

Be and Act as Priests!

- As we proclaim our sonship given us by Baptism, so we are to proclaim our priesthood given us by Ordination.
- We *are* priests—Proclaim it.
    Be explicit. Be clear about it. It is a heavenly ministry, in union with Christ our High Priest,

by His choice, by His calling and by His power.
- Therefore we need to *act* as priests.
    Offer sacrifice with fervor.
    Intercede with boldness.
    Fight the heavenly battle, humbly, with the power of the Holy Spirit.
    Invoke the Holy Spirit constantly.
    —We need an intense and immense *epiklesis!*
- We are both ministers and mystery.
    We are not *just* ministers, or enablers, or catalysts, or promoters or charisms, or presiders over the assembly,
    We are *priests* in Christ our High Priest.

The Priest is both minister and mystery:

He *serves as minister of:*
- Glory—glorifying the Father and man in Christ;
- Eucharist and Reconciliation—giving self in Christ and forgiving sins;
- The Living Word—proclaiming Jesus Christ in the power of the Holy Spirit;
- Mercy—a man of mercy and a vessel of mercy;
- Redemption—paying the price of *sin*;
- Power of the Holy Spirit—saving, healing, delivering.

He *lives the mystery of*—
- Christ—as sacrament of Christ;
- Glory of the Father, Son and Holy Spirit;
- Eucharist and Reconciliation;
- Redemptive—Incarnation;
- MERCY!—Mercy Incarnate;
- Marriage to Christ and His Church;
- Mary—virginal yet espoused and fruitful;
- Church and Kingdom—as ready and not yet.

All this is the Mystery of Mercy and Mary—all this is gift! So we need to ask for the Holy Spirit to "Renew within us the Spirit of holiness" (words of ordination to the priesthood, Roman Rite).

Come, Holy Spirit, make me a priest after the Heart of Jesus. Come, Holy Spirit, make me a living icon of the merciful Jesus. Come, Holy Spirit, fill me with mercy that I may be a minister of mercy, the mystery of mercy incarnate like Jesus. Come, Holy Spirit, spouse of Mary, purify me, fill me, possess me and transform me and conform me to Christ Jesus, High Priest and Mercy Incarnate.

> In Jesus our merciful High Priest and Mary, Mother of Mercy,
> Fr. George

35. AN EPILOGUE: GOD'S FASCINATING WAYS

December 10, 1985
Holy Family Hermitage

Dear Father Ed,

After rereading all these letters as a unit and then reflecting on what else the Lord has been doing, I became aware of the various and fascinating ways He has of relating to me and I would presume that many of these apply to all of us priests.

- God is mystery; I am mystery! I don't understand God and I don't understand myself. Put the two together and we have mystery compounded to the nth degree! This is the fascinating reality of relating to God. There is no limit to seeking and searching to understand and to love Him. He is infinite, wonderful and fabulous and He has all eternity to reveal Himself to us. He has created me free to freely choose Him and this is my mystery. I will only find out who I am in the mystery of God Who made me for Himself.

- My relationship with the Lord is always new. He has an infinite variety of ways of relating and communicating, which calls for a fresh seeking of Him daily. At the heart of the issue is the free act of the will seeking Him, trusting Him, loving Him, submitting to Him. There is no formula for this—not even for a biochemist! Lord, may I have the gift of discernment so that my heart can recognize You always. Now I appreciate even more the words of Pope Paul VI addressed to a group of thirteen of us in October, 1973, "Discernment is the gift of gifts!"

- God really is a God of surprises. He has a unique sense of humor; and the best way to respond to some of the situations I find myself in, is a good hearty laugh. After all, He is God and He is in charge; He is Creator and Savior; He is almighty and omnipresent; He is merciful with a tenderness to a point of "weakness." The Father as the Giver of all good gifts has more gifts and surprises for us than we can ask or imagine.

- God has His own sense of timing. I wear a wrist watch, God doesn't. He is the God of eternity and all time is *now* to Him. What has already happened in Heaven, is yet to happen on earth. This is what we pray in the Lord's prayer; this is what we read in the Book of Revelation. All this totally different concept of time and timing calls for waiting upon the Lord, enduring patiently, and staying alert and praying. He comes at the most unexpected moments!—even to the point of embarrassment. The Lord wants us to live with the expectancy of His coming today.

- Everything, but everything is a lesson for me to learn and an occasion to trust in the Lord. God is God always and everywhere so there is no such thing as an accident. All things are under His providential care. So really, I must "Rejoice always. Pray without ceasing. In all things give thanks" (*1 Thess.* 5:16-18, Confraternity Edition).

- God is infinitely merciful. I have known His faithful and steadfast love for me throughout my whole life. As I looked over my life during these days of solitude, I was amazed at how faithful the Lord has been to me, especially as I went down the wrong paths. My heart overflows with thanksgiving that He knew and cared for me. The words of St. Paul to the Galatians came alive "(He) loved me and gave Himself for me: (*Gal.* 2:20b). My amazement continues to grow as I see His mercy at work in me during these days of solitude.

- The Lord comes in gentle breezes, as well as in the mighty winds. A movement of the Lord, a grace, a prompting, an insight, comes and goes. If one is alert to it and listens to it, it can become a mighty whirlwind. But these gentle breezes sometimes come by only once. If not detected, they pass by and we miss out on a great grace. The breeze might be a gentle word in the heart, an occasion of meeting a person, or a memory of a person coming to mind. Each will evoke a different need and a different response—but all of them call for intercession: "Jesus! Mercy!"

- For many years, "ups and downs" have been a pattern in my life. But now I see them as the Lord's way to keep me humble. After an uplifting grace I can prepare for a "downer"—after the exhortation of St. Ignatius of Loyola, who said that in consolation we should prepare for desolation. Humility is needed always and everywhere; and humiliations are the best way to grow in humility, again according to St. Ignatius. I've realized that I'm like a Yo-Yo, up and down, but I've come to realize too that I'm the Lord's Yo-Yo and He delights in me.

    Related to the "ups and downs" is the reality that I am a sinner—especially when I don't reflect that I am. I am always in need of the Lord's saving mercy. Jesus! Mercy!

In all of this I find, as I have mentioned in an earlier letter, that I'm like a butterfly. I was reading Carmen Bernos de Gasztold's "Prayer from the Ark," (Viking Press, NY, 1962), which gives the prayers of various animals on Noah's Ark. It is a delightful collection of prayers that captures the character of so many animals. I identified with the butterfly, flitting and fluttering from one thing to another, but I realized that I am the Lord's butterfly. I am a royal butterfly—I'm a "mysterious monarch."

> In the Mercy of our Lord Jesus Christ,
> Fr. George

FAITH PUBLISHING COMPANY

Faith Publishing Company has been organized as a service for the publishing and distribution of materials that reflect Christian values, and in particular the teachings of the Catholic Church.

It is dedicated to publication of only those materials that reflect such values.

For further information, or additional copies of this book, contact:

Faith Publishing Company
P.O. Box 237
Milford, Ohio 45150